Mastering
COMPUTER VIRUSES AND ANTIVIRUSES
Concepts, Techniques, and Applications

Nikhilesh Mishra,
Author

Website
https://www.nikhileshmishra.com

Copyright Information

i

Dedication

This book is lovingly dedicated to the cherished memory of my father, **Late Krishna Gopal Mishra**, and my mother, **Mrs. Vijay Kanti Mishra.** Their unwavering support, guidance, and love continue to inspire me.

Table of Contents

Chapter 8   **154**

Chapter 9   **177**

Chapter 10   **202**

Author's Preface

Welcome to the captivating world of the knowledge we are about to explore! Within these pages, we invite you to embark on a journey that delves into the frontiers of information and understanding.

Charting the Path to Knowledge

Dive deep into the subjects we are about to explore as we unravel the intricate threads of innovation, creativity, and problem-solving. Whether you're a curious enthusiast, a seasoned professional, or an eager learner, this book serves as your gateway to gaining a deeper understanding.

Your Guiding Light

From the foundational principles of our chosen field to the advanced frontiers of its applications, we've meticulously crafted this book to be your trusted companion. Each chapter is an expedition, guided by expertise and filled with practical insights to empower you on your quest for knowledge.

What Awaits You

- **Illuminate the Origins:** Embark on a journey through the historical evolution of our chosen field, discovering key milestones that have paved the way for breakthroughs.

- **Demystify Complex Concepts:** Grasp the fundamental principles, navigate intricate concepts, and explore practical applications.

- **Mastery of the Craft:** Equip yourself with the skills and knowledge needed to excel in our chosen domain.

Your Journey Begins Here

As we embark on this enlightening journey together, remember that mastery is not just about knowledge but also the wisdom to apply it. Let each chapter be a stepping stone towards unlocking your potential, and let this book be your guide to becoming a true connoisseur of our chosen field.

So, turn the page, delve into the chapters, and immerse yourself in the world of knowledge. Let curiosity be your compass, and let the pursuit of understanding be your guide.

Begin your expedition now. Your quest for mastery awaits!

Sincerely,

Nikhilesh Mishra,

Author

CHAPTER 1

Understanding Computer Viruses

In today's interconnected digital world, understanding computer viruses is paramount to safeguarding our data, privacy, and the integrity of the systems we rely on daily. Computer viruses are not mere lines of malicious code; they are sophisticated threats that have evolved over decades, posing ever-present challenges to cybersecurity. In this chapter, we embark on a journey to dissect and demystify these digital adversaries, equipping you with the knowledge needed to defend against their insidious attacks.

A. Defining Computer Viruses and Malware

In the realm of cybersecurity, the terms "computer viruses" and "malware" are frequently used, often interchangeably, but they represent distinct categories of malicious software. To truly understand the threats they pose and how to protect against them, it's essential to dissect these definitions and recognize their nuances.

1. Computer Viruses: The Silent Invaders

A computer virus is a type of malicious software that operates like a biological virus in many ways. Just as a biological virus can infect a host organism and replicate itself, a computer virus can infect a computer system and replicate within it. However, unlike biological viruses, computer viruses don't have a life of their own. Instead, they are pieces of code or software that attach themselves to legitimate programs or files, effectively hijacking these programs to execute their malicious actions.

Key characteristics of computer viruses include:

- **Replication**: A defining feature of viruses is their ability to reproduce and spread. Once a virus infects a host file or program, it can propagate to other files or systems when the infected program is executed or shared.

- **Payload**: Computer viruses often carry a payload, which is the harmful action they are designed to perform. This action can vary widely, from deleting files to stealing sensitive data or even rendering the infected system inoperable.

- **Concealment**: Viruses are notorious for their ability to hide within legitimate files, making detection challenging. They can also employ various techniques to avoid detection by antivirus software.

2. Malware: A Broader Category

Malware is a broader category that encompasses various types of malicious software, including computer viruses. While viruses are a specific subset of malware, malware as a whole covers a wide spectrum of malicious programs designed to harm or compromise computer systems, networks, and data.

Types of malware include:

•   **Worms**: Worms are self-replicating programs that spread across networks, often exploiting vulnerabilities to infect other computers. Unlike viruses, worms do not need to attach themselves to existing files.

•   **Trojans**: Named after the legendary Trojan Horse, Trojans are deceptive malware that masquerade as legitimate software. Once inside a system, they open a backdoor for attackers, allowing unauthorized access.

•   **Ransomware**: Ransomware is a type of malware that encrypts a victim's files, rendering them inaccessible. Attackers demand a ransom to provide the decryption key, often in cryptocurrency.

•   **Spyware**: Spyware is designed to stealthily monitor a user's activities, including keystrokes, web browsing, and personal data, which is then transmitted to a remote server.

- **Adware**: Adware inundates users with unwanted advertisements and can collect information about their browsing habits to serve targeted ads.

- **Rootkits**: Rootkits are particularly stealthy malware that can hide their presence and provide unauthorized access to a computer system, often giving attackers elevated privileges.

Understanding the distinctions between computer viruses and other forms of malware is crucial because it influences how cybersecurity professionals detect, prevent, and mitigate these threats. While viruses are one of the oldest and most iconic forms of malware, the landscape has evolved to include a vast array of malicious software with distinct behaviors and attack vectors. Recognizing these nuances is the first step in building effective defenses against the ever-evolving threats posed by the digital underworld.

B. Anatomy of a Virus: Dissecting the Malicious Code

Understanding the anatomy of a computer virus is akin to examining the inner workings of a sophisticated criminal enterprise. A computer virus, like its biological counterpart, has a well-defined structure and components that enable it to infiltrate, propagate, and execute its malicious payload. To defend against these insidious digital invaders, one must comprehend the intricate details of their composition.

1. The Outer Shell: Infection Mechanism

At the core of every computer virus is its infection mechanism. This is the initial entry point into a host system. The virus must find a way to enter the target system, whether through user actions, software vulnerabilities, or other means. The outer shell contains the code responsible for infecting host files, programs, or even boot sectors, depending on the virus type.

• **Infection Vectors**: Viruses use various infection vectors to infiltrate systems. These may include email attachments, malicious downloads, infected USB drives, or even exploiting software vulnerabilities. For instance, email-borne viruses rely on users opening infected attachments or clicking on malicious links.

2. The Genetic Code: Virus Payload

The genetic code of a computer virus resides in its payload. This is the part of the virus that carries out its malicious intent. The payload can take numerous forms, depending on the virus's purpose and design.

• **Data Corruption**: Some viruses are engineered to corrupt or destroy data, rendering files and systems unusable. This is often seen in file-infecting viruses that overwrite or delete critical data.

- **Data Theft**: Other viruses, particularly spyware or information-stealing malware, are designed to exfiltrate sensitive data, such as personal information, login credentials, or financial details.

- **Ransomware**: In the case of ransomware, the payload encrypts a victim's files, and the attacker demands a ransom in exchange for the decryption key.

- **Backdoor Access**: Viruses can establish backdoor access to infected systems, allowing attackers to gain unauthorized control over the compromised computer.

3. The Genetic Code: Triggers and Activation

Within the payload, viruses often include triggers and activation mechanisms. These are conditions or events that determine when and how the virus executes its malicious code. For instance:

- **Time-Based Activation**: Some viruses are programmed to activate on specific dates or after a certain amount of time has passed since infection.

- **User Interaction**: Viruses can be triggered when a user performs a particular action, such as opening an infected file or running an infected program.

- **Remote Commands**: In the case of remote-controlled botnet viruses, the virus may wait for commands from a remote attacker before initiating its activities.

4. Self-Replication: The Propagation Engine

A fundamental characteristic of viruses is their ability to self-replicate. This is achieved through a replication engine embedded within the virus's code. The replication engine allows the virus to create copies of itself and spread to other files, systems, or networks.

- **Infection Methods**: Viruses can employ various infection methods, such as appending their code to existing files, injecting code into system processes, or exploiting vulnerabilities to gain control of a target system.

5. Stealth Mechanisms: Evasion Techniques

To evade detection by antivirus software and security mechanisms, viruses often employ stealth techniques. These include:

- **Polymorphism**: Some viruses constantly modify their code, making each infection appear unique and evading signature-based detection.

- **Encryption**: Encrypting their code or communication channels can prevent easy analysis and detection.

- **Rootkit Integration**: Viruses may integrate with rootkits to hide their presence and make detection even more challenging.

Understanding the anatomy of a virus is essential for cybersecurity professionals tasked with identifying and mitigating these threats. By dissecting a virus's components, one can develop effective countermeasures and enhance security protocols to protect against the ever-evolving landscape of malicious software.

C. Historical Evolution of Computer Viruses: From Curiosity to Cyber Threat

The history of computer viruses is a fascinating journey through the evolution of technology, programming, and cybersecurity. These malicious entities, initially born as experiments and pranks, have transformed into formidable cyber threats with significant societal and economic impacts. To understand their evolution is to comprehend the continuous battle between malicious actors and defenders in the digital age.

1. The Dawn of Computing: Conceptual Beginnings (1940s-1960s)

The roots of computer viruses can be traced back to the early days of computing, primarily during the development of mainframe computers in the mid-20th century. At this stage:

- **Conceptual Origins**: The idea of self-replicating programs emerged as a theoretical concept rather than a malicious intent. Pioneering computer scientists like John von Neumann discussed the possibility of self-replicating automata.

2. Emergence of Pranks: The Creeper and Reaper (1970s)

The first documented instance of a computer program exhibiting virus-like behavior was the Creeper virus. Developed in the early 1970s, Creeper was more of an experiment than a malicious act. It displayed a message on infected computers, saying, "I'm the creeper, catch me if you can!" The Reaper program was then created to "catch" and remove Creeper from infected systems, marking an early attempt at antivirus software.

3. The Birth of Malicious Intent (1980s)

The 1980s witnessed the shift from experimentation to malicious intent. Key developments during this period include:

- **1982 - Elk Cloner**: Elk Cloner, written by a high school student named Rich Skrenta, is considered one of the first computer viruses to infect Apple II computers. It was relatively harmless, displaying a humorous message, but it highlighted the potential for mischief in the digital world.

- **1983 - Brain**: Brain, the first IBM PC virus, emerged in Pakistan. It spread via infected floppy disks and was intended to protect against unauthorized copying. It marked the beginning of viruses targeting personal computers.

4. The Proliferation of PC Viruses (1980s-1990s)

The 1980s and 1990s saw a surge in the number and complexity of computer viruses:

- **File-Infecting Viruses**: Viruses like Vienna and Cascade demonstrated the ability to infect executable files, making them more potent and challenging to detect.

- **Polymorphism**: Viruses like Tequila and Dark Avenger introduced polymorphic techniques, changing their code with each infection to evade signature-based detection.

- **Internet and Email**: The advent of the internet and email provided new infection vectors, leading to viruses like Melissa (1999) and ILOVEYOU (2000) that spread rapidly through email attachments.

5. The Rise of Worms and Blended Threats (2000s)

The early 2000s saw the emergence of worms like Code Red and Nimda, which exploited network vulnerabilities to spread rapidly. This era also witnessed the rise of blended threats, combining viruses, worms, Trojans, and other malware components to maximize damage.

6. Modern Malware Landscape (2010s-2020s)

The evolution of computer viruses continued into the 2010s and beyond, marked by:

• **Ransomware**: The emergence of ransomware families like CryptoLocker (2013) and WannaCry (2017), which encrypted files and demanded ransoms.

• **Advanced Persistent Threats (APTs)**: State-sponsored actors and cybercriminal groups increasingly utilized APTs, combining sophisticated malware with targeted strategies for espionage and data theft.

• **Fileless Malware and Nation-State Attacks**: Newer threats, such as fileless malware and nation-state attacks like Stuxnet (2010), demonstrated the next level of sophistication in cyber-espionage and sabotage.

• **AI and Machine Learning**: Malware authors started leveraging artificial intelligence and machine learning for evasion and evasion-resistant techniques.

The historical evolution of computer viruses showcases a progression from simple experiments to complex, highly targeted threats. As technology advances, viruses adapt and exploit new vulnerabilities. This ongoing cat-and-mouse game underscores the critical importance of cybersecurity measures, antivirus software, and user education to mitigate the risks posed by these ever-evolving digital adversaries. The journey of computer viruses is a testament to the continuous innovation and adaptation that characterizes the world of cybersecurity.

D. The Cybersecurity Landscape: Navigating the Digital Battleground

In today's interconnected world, the cybersecurity landscape has become a critical battleground where individuals, organizations, and nations defend against an evolving array of digital threats. Understanding this complex and dynamic landscape is essential for effectively protecting data, privacy, and the integrity of systems in an age where cyberattacks have far-reaching consequences.

1. The Pervasiveness of Technology

The cybersecurity landscape is shaped by the ubiquity of technology. In the digital age, technology is deeply integrated into every aspect of our lives, from personal communications and financial transactions to critical infrastructure and national defense. The proliferation of devices, interconnected systems, and the Internet of Things (IoT) has expanded the attack surface, providing more opportunities for cybercriminals and nation-states to exploit vulnerabilities.

2. The Threat Actors

The cybersecurity landscape is inhabited by various threat actors, each with distinct motives and capabilities:

- **Cybercriminals**: These individuals or groups are motivated by financial gain. They launch attacks like ransomware, data theft, and fraud to monetize their activities.

- **Nation-States**: State-sponsored actors engage in cyber espionage, sabotage, and cyber warfare to further national interests. Examples include Stuxnet, a malware designed to disrupt Iran's nuclear program, and APT29 (Cozy Bear), linked to Russian intelligence.

- **Hacktivists**: Hacktivists target organizations or governments to promote a social or political cause. They deface websites, leak sensitive data, or disrupt online services to draw attention to their agendas.

- **Insiders**: Insiders with privileged access to systems can pose a significant threat. They may steal data, introduce malware, or intentionally compromise security.

3. Attack Vectors and Techniques

Cyberattacks come in various forms, and attackers continuously innovate to overcome defenses. Common attack vectors and techniques include:

- **Phishing**: Attackers impersonate trusted entities to trick individuals into revealing sensitive information or clicking on malicious links.

- **Malware**: Malicious software includes viruses, worms, Trojans, and ransomware. Malware can infect systems, steal data, or encrypt files for extortion.

- **Zero-Day Exploits**: Attackers target vulnerabilities in software or hardware that are not yet known to the vendor. These exploits are difficult to defend against until patches are developed.

- **Distributed Denial of Service (DDoS)**: Attackers flood a target's network or website with traffic to overwhelm it and disrupt services.

4. Security Technologies and Strategies

To navigate the cybersecurity landscape, organizations and individuals deploy a range of security technologies and strategies:

- **Firewalls and Intrusion Detection/Prevention Systems**: These technologies monitor network traffic and block suspicious activity.

- **Antivirus and Anti-Malware Software**: These tools detect and remove malicious software.

- **Encryption**: Encrypting data ensures that even if it is intercepted, it remains unreadable without the decryption key.

- **Multi-Factor Authentication (MFA)**: MFA adds an extra layer of security by requiring multiple forms of verification to access accounts.

- **Security Awareness Training**: Educating users about cybersecurity best practices helps prevent social engineering attacks.

5. Regulatory and Legal Frameworks

The cybersecurity landscape is also influenced by regulatory and legal frameworks. Governments worldwide are enacting laws and regulations to protect data and hold organizations accountable for security breaches. Examples include the European Union's General Data Protection Regulation (GDPR) and the California Consumer Privacy Act (CCPA).

6. Emerging Threats and Technologies

The landscape continues to evolve as emerging technologies like artificial intelligence and quantum computing present both new opportunities and challenges. Cybersecurity professionals must adapt to these changes, harnessing AI for threat detection and preparing for the potential cryptographic vulnerabilities posed by quantum computing.

7. Collaboration and Information Sharing

In response to the dynamic nature of the cybersecurity landscape, collaboration and information sharing among organizations, governments, and cybersecurity experts are crucial. Initiatives such as threat intelligence sharing and the establishment of Computer Emergency Response Teams (CERTs) foster collective defense against cyber threats.

Understanding the cybersecurity landscape is an ongoing endeavor, as it requires staying informed about emerging threats, implementing robust security measures, and fostering a culture of cybersecurity awareness. As technology continues to advance, the battleground will shift, but the importance of securing the digital realm remains constant, making cybersecurity a perpetual challenge and priority in the modern world.

Chapter 2

Types and Categories of Malware

In the ever-evolving landscape of cybersecurity, an essential foundation lies in understanding the diverse ecosystem of malware – malicious software engineered with various intents. These digital adversaries come in many forms, each with its unique traits and objectives. In this chapter, we embark on a journey to explore the intricate world of malware, categorizing its types and shedding light on the multifaceted threats that lurk within the digital realm.

A. Categories of Malware: Viruses, Worms, Trojans

The world of malware is teeming with a diverse range of malicious software, each designed with specific purposes and techniques. Understanding the categories of malware is crucial for identifying, mitigating, and defending against these digital threats. In this section, we delve deep into three prominent categories: viruses, worms, and Trojans.

1. Viruses: The Digital Parasites

Computer viruses are among the most well-known and

historically significant forms of malware. Like their biological counterparts, computer viruses are parasitic entities that rely on a host to survive and propagate. Here's an in-depth look at computer viruses:

- **Infection Mechanism**: Viruses attach themselves to legitimate files or programs, effectively hiding within them. When the infected file is executed, the virus activates, seeking new hosts to infect.

- **Replication**: A defining feature of viruses is their ability to replicate. They can spread to other files or systems through infected files, email attachments, or infected media.

- **Payload**: Viruses carry a payload, which is the malicious action they are programmed to perform. This can range from data corruption to stealing sensitive information or rendering the infected system inoperable.

- **Evolution**: Over the years, viruses have evolved to include polymorphic capabilities, enabling them to change their code with each infection to evade signature-based detection.

2. Worms: The Network Spreaders

Computer worms share similarities with viruses but have distinct characteristics, primarily revolving around their method of propagation and behavior:

- **Self-Replication**: Worms, like viruses, have the ability to replicate themselves, but they don't rely on attaching to files. Instead, they exploit network vulnerabilities or security weaknesses to propagate independently.

- **Rapid Spread**: Worms can spread rapidly across networks, infecting multiple systems within a short period. Their ability to self-replicate without user intervention makes them highly effective at spreading.

- **Payload**: Worms often carry a payload that can vary widely, from data destruction to creating backdoors for remote access.

- **Notable Worms**: Notable examples include the Morris Worm (1988), which was one of the earliest worms to cause significant damage, and the Conficker worm (2008), which exploited Windows vulnerabilities to infect millions of computers globally.

3. Trojans: The Deceptive Intruders

Trojan horses, often referred to as Trojans, derive their name from the Greek myth of the wooden horse used to infiltrate Troy. Trojans, like their namesake, disguise themselves as legitimate and benign software to gain entry into a system:

- **Deception**: Trojans often masquerade as legitimate

programs or files, enticing users to download or execute them.

- **Backdoor Access**: Once inside a system, Trojans can open a backdoor, providing unauthorized access to attackers.

- **Diverse Payloads**: Trojans can have a wide range of malicious payloads, including data theft, remote control, or the delivery of additional malware.

- **RATs and Banking Trojans**: Remote Access Trojans (RATs) allow attackers to control infected systems remotely, while banking Trojans target financial information and transactions.

Understanding these categories of malware is foundational for both cybersecurity professionals and individuals seeking to protect their systems and data. It empowers defenders to recognize the telltale signs of infection, employ appropriate mitigation strategies, and stay vigilant in the ongoing battle against digital threats in the modern age.

B. File-Infecting Viruses: The Stealthy Manipulators

File-infecting viruses represent a category of malware that has been a persistent and evolving threat in the world of cybersecurity. These digital adversaries are characterized by their ability to attach themselves to legitimate files or programs, effectively hiding within them like a parasite. In this in-depth exploration, we delve into the intricate world of file-infecting viruses, understanding their mechanisms, historical significance, and the challenges they pose to cybersecurity.

1. Mechanisms of File-Infecting Viruses

File-infecting viruses, often referred to simply as "file infectors," are a subset of computer viruses with distinct characteristics:

- **Attachment to Legitimate Files**: Unlike some other types of malware that operate independently, file infectors attach themselves to existing, legitimate files or programs. This camouflage allows them to go undetected for extended periods.

- **Infection Process**: When an infected file is executed, the virus activates and embeds its code into the host file. The file is now compromised, serving as a carrier for the virus.

- **Stealth Techniques**: File infectors employ various techniques to evade detection. They may modify the host file's code, making it appear unchanged upon cursory inspection. Additionally, some file infectors employ polymorphic or metamorphic capabilities, altering their code with each infection to thwart signature-based antivirus detection.

2. Historical Significance

File-infecting viruses hold historical significance in the evolution of malware and cybersecurity:

- **Early Examples**: Some of the earliest computer viruses, like the Vienna virus (1987) on the Amiga platform, were file infectors. They demonstrated the concept of infecting executable files, paving the way for future generations of viruses.

- **Boot Sector Viruses**: A subset of file infectors known as boot sector viruses infect the Master Boot Record (MBR) of a storage device, compromising the system's ability to boot. Examples include the notorious Michelangelo virus (1991).

- **Macro Viruses**: In the 1990s and early 2000s, macro viruses targeted productivity software like Microsoft Word and Excel. The Melissa virus (1999) and the Concept virus (2001) exploited macros within documents, illustrating the adaptability of file infectors.

3. Payload and Intent

File-infecting viruses can carry a wide range of payloads and have diverse intents:

- **Data Corruption**: Some file infectors are programmed to corrupt or destroy data within infected files, rendering them unusable.

- **Replication**: A core characteristic is replication. Infected files are carriers, allowing the virus to spread to other files on the same system or to external devices when files are shared.

- **Additional Malware Delivery**: File infectors may serve as a delivery mechanism for additional malware components, expanding the scope of the attack.

- **Botnet Formation**: In some cases, file infectors are used to create botnets, networks of infected computers controlled by a remote attacker.

4. Mitigation and Defense

Mitigating file-infecting viruses requires a multi-faceted approach:

- **Antivirus Software**: Robust antivirus software is essential for detecting and removing file infectors. Regularly updating antivirus signatures is crucial to staying protected.

- **Regular Backups**: Frequent backups of important files can mitigate the impact of data corruption caused by file infectors.

- **User Education**: Training users to recognize suspicious files and avoid downloading or executing unknown attachments is vital in preventing infections.

- **Patch Management**: Keeping operating systems and software up-to-date with security patches can prevent some file infections, as they often exploit known vulnerabilities.

File-infecting viruses represent a fascinating and enduring chapter in the history of cybersecurity. As they continue to adapt and evolve, cybersecurity professionals must remain vigilant, employ advanced detection techniques, and educate users to defend against these stealthy manipulators effectively.

C. Boot Sector Viruses: Infecting the Heart of the System

Boot sector viruses represent a notorious category of malware that targets a fundamental component of computer systems—the boot sector. These malicious entities have played a significant role in the history of computer viruses, causing widespread damage and disruption. In this in-depth exploration, we delve into the intricate world of boot sector viruses, examining their mechanisms, historical significance, and the challenges they pose to cybersecurity.

1. Anatomy of Boot Sector Viruses

Boot sector viruses are named for their primary target—the Master Boot Record (MBR) or the boot sector of storage devices like hard drives, floppy disks, and, more recently, SSDs. Here's a closer look at their mechanisms:

- **Infection Point**: Boot sector viruses typically reside in the boot sector of a storage device, waiting for the system to boot. When the infected storage device is accessed, the virus activates.

- **Infection Process**: During the boot-up sequence, the virus loads into memory and takes control of the system's boot process. It may also write a legitimate MBR code to a different location on the disk to maintain functionality.

- **Payload**: Like other viruses, boot sector viruses can carry payloads, which can include data destruction, data theft, or the delivery of additional malware.

- **Propagation**: Boot sector viruses can spread to other storage devices when infected disks are used on different computers. For instance, an infected floppy disk can introduce the virus to multiple systems.

2. Historical Significance

Boot sector viruses hold historical significance in the world of computer viruses and cybersecurity:

- **Early Examples**: One of the earliest examples is the Brain virus (1986), which targeted IBM PC-compatible computers. It displayed a message and contact information but did not cause significant harm.

- **Michelangelo**: The Michelangelo virus (1991) garnered significant attention due to its potential to destroy data on infected systems on March 6th, the artist Michelangelo's birthday.

- **Chernobyl (CIH) Virus**: Also known as the CIH virus, it caused widespread damage in 1998 by overwriting the BIOS of infected computers, rendering them inoperable.

3. Impact and Challenges

Boot sector viruses pose unique challenges and can have severe consequences:

- **Data Loss**: In cases where boot sector viruses overwrite or corrupt data, users may experience data loss and system instability.

- **Boot Failure**: Some boot sector viruses can prevent systems from booting, rendering them unusable until the MBR is repaired.

- **Persistence**: Boot sector viruses can be challenging to remove, as they often reside in an area of the storage device that standard antivirus software may not readily access.

4. Mitigation and Defense

Effectively mitigating boot sector viruses requires proactive measures and recovery strategies:

•   **Boot from Read-Only Media**: Booting from read-only media, like a write-protected CD or USB drive, can prevent boot sector viruses from infecting the system.

•   **Regular Backups**: Frequent backups of critical data can mitigate the impact of data loss caused by boot sector viruses.

•   **BIOS Security**: Protecting the BIOS with a password can prevent unauthorized changes, such as those attempted by some boot sector viruses.

•   **Antivirus Software**: Advanced antivirus software can detect and remove boot sector viruses. Some tools also provide boot-time scanning to address these threats.

Boot sector viruses represent a fascinating yet challenging aspect of cybersecurity history. While their prominence has waned in the face of more advanced threats, understanding their mechanisms and adopting proactive defense measures remains essential to protect against these malicious entities that target the heart of computer systems.

D. Macro Viruses: Exploiting Productivity Software

Macro viruses represent a unique and historically significant category of malware that capitalizes on the functionality of productivity software, such as word processors and spreadsheet applications. These viruses have posed substantial threats in the past, leveraging the macros embedded in documents to spread and execute malicious code. In this comprehensive exploration, we delve into the intricate world of macro viruses, understanding their mechanisms, historical significance, and their place in modern cybersecurity.

1. Anatomy of Macro Viruses

Macro viruses are a subset of malware with distinct characteristics, primarily revolving around their utilization of macros, which are sequences of instructions in a scripting or programming language. Here's a closer look at their mechanisms:

- **Infection Point**: Macro viruses are typically embedded within documents created using productivity software like Microsoft Word, Excel, or PowerPoint. These viruses rely on users opening infected documents.

- **Activation Process**: When an infected document is opened, the macro virus's code is executed, often with the user's permission or inadvertently. The virus then typically takes control of the host application and may replicate itself to other documents.

- **Payload**: Macro viruses can carry payloads that range from data corruption to delivering additional malware. Some are designed to spread rapidly, while others focus on specific malicious actions.

- **Social Engineering**: Macro viruses often rely on social engineering tactics to trick users into enabling macros, such as by presenting enticing content or posing as legitimate documents.

2. Historical Significance

Macro viruses have played a significant role in the history of malware and cybersecurity:

- **Early Examples**: One of the earliest macro viruses, Concept (1995), targeted Microsoft Word. It spread via infected Word documents and demonstrated the potential for macros to be exploited maliciously.

- **Melissa**: The Melissa virus (1999) gained notoriety for its rapid spread via infected Word documents sent as email attachments. It disrupted email services and highlighted the vulnerability of Microsoft Office applications.

3. Impact and Challenges

Macro viruses have posed unique challenges and can have a substantial impact:

- **Data Corruption**: Some macro viruses are

programmed to corrupt data within documents, rendering them unreadable or unusable.

- **Rapid Spread**: The ability of macro viruses to spread via infected documents, often through email, has made them a potent vector for cyberattacks.

- **Social Engineering**: The reliance on social engineering tactics means that users' actions play a pivotal role in the success of macro virus infections.

4. Mitigation and Defense

Mitigating macro viruses requires a combination of user education, security best practices, and technological measures:

- **Disable Macros**: A proactive approach is to disable macros by default in productivity software and only enable them in documents from trusted sources.

- **User Education**: Training users to recognize and avoid opening suspicious attachments or enabling macros is vital.

- **Antivirus Software**: Modern antivirus software includes macro virus detection and removal capabilities.

- **Document Inspection**: Some email and content filtering solutions can inspect documents for macro viruses before they reach users' inboxes.

Macro viruses may have been more prominent in the past, but they remain a part of the malware landscape. Understanding their mechanisms and implementing appropriate defenses is essential to protect against these threats that exploit the very tools we use for productivity and communication.

E. Ransomware, Spyware, and More: Exploring the Spectrum of Malicious Software

The world of malware is vast and multifaceted, encompassing a broad spectrum of malicious software designed to achieve various objectives, from financial gain to espionage. In this comprehensive exploration, we delve into some prominent categories of malware, shedding light on their mechanisms, motivations, and the challenges they pose to cybersecurity.

1. Ransomware: The Digital Extortionists

Ransomware is a malicious software category that has gained notoriety for its ability to encrypt files and demand a ransom for decryption. Here's an in-depth look at ransomware:

• **Infection and Encryption**: Ransomware infects a victim's system, encrypts files using strong encryption algorithms, and demands a ransom in exchange for the decryption key.

• **Motivation**: Ransomware operators seek financial

gain, targeting individuals, businesses, and even critical infrastructure. High-profile ransomware attacks have highlighted their disruptive potential.

- **Variants**: Ransomware comes in various forms, including crypto-ransomware, which encrypts files, and locker-ransomware, which locks users out of their systems.

- **Notable Examples**: Notable ransomware strains include WannaCry, NotPetya, and Ryuk, each with its unique methods and objectives.

2. Spyware: The Silent Observers

Spyware is a category of malware designed to monitor and gather information from infected systems, often without the victim's knowledge. Here's a closer look at spyware:

- **Information Gathering**: Spyware can capture keystrokes, record browsing habits, collect personal information, and even remotely activate a device's camera or microphone.

- **Motivation**: Spyware is often used for surveillance, data theft, or corporate espionage. Some spyware is deployed by governments for intelligence purposes.

- **Delivery Methods**: Spyware can be delivered through malicious email attachments, infected websites, or bundled with seemingly legitimate software.

- **Prevalence**: Spyware remains a pervasive threat, particularly in the context of personal privacy and corporate espionage.

3. Adware: The Unwanted Advertisers

Adware is a category of software that generates unwanted advertisements on a user's device, often in the form of pop-up ads or browser redirects:

- **Monetization**: Adware generates revenue for its creators by displaying advertisements. In some cases, it may track user behavior to deliver targeted ads.

- **Distribution**: Adware can be bundled with legitimate software or distributed through deceptive advertisements or compromised websites.

- **User Experience**: Adware can degrade system performance, disrupt browsing, and compromise user privacy.

4. Rootkits: The Stealthy Infiltrators

Rootkits are a type of malware that grant unauthorized access and control over a victim's system while hiding their presence:

- **Evasion**: Rootkits often employ stealth techniques to hide their presence from security software and even the operating system itself.

- **Privilege Escalation**: Once installed, rootkits can escalate their privileges, giving attackers complete control over the compromised system.

- **Purpose**: Rootkits can be used for various malicious activities, including data theft, remote control, and maintaining persistent access to a system.

5. Trojan Horses: The Deceptive Intruders

Trojan horses, commonly known as Trojans, are malware that masquerade as legitimate software to deceive users into executing them:

- **Deception**: Trojans often disguise themselves as useful or benign software to trick users into downloading and running them.

- **Payload**: Trojans can carry a wide range of malicious payloads, including backdoors for remote access, data theft capabilities, or the delivery of additional malware.

- **Use Cases**: Trojans are versatile and can be employed for various purposes, from data theft to enabling remote control of infected systems.

Understanding the diverse landscape of malware is essential for cybersecurity professionals and individuals seeking to protect their systems and data. Each category of malware presents unique challenges and requires tailored defense strategies to mitigate the risks they pose in the ever-evolving world of cyber threats.

Chapter 3

How Viruses Spread

In the intricate world of computer viruses, understanding how these digital adversaries spread is paramount to fortifying one's defenses. This chapter delves into the various infection vectors and techniques that viruses employ to propagate, unveiling the strategies that cybercriminals and malware authors employ to infiltrate systems and networks, often with devastating consequences.

A. Infection Vectors: Unveiling the Gateways of Computer Viruses

Computer viruses are crafty adversaries, employing a variety of infection vectors to infiltrate systems and networks. These infection pathways, often exploited by cybercriminals and malware authors, are the gateways through which viruses spread and propagate. In this comprehensive exploration, we delve into the intricate world of infection vectors, understanding the strategies used by computer viruses to gain access to target systems.

1. Email: The Trojan Horse of the Digital Age

Email remains one of the most common and effective infection vectors for computer viruses:

- **Phishing Emails**: Cybercriminals craft convincing emails that appear legitimate, enticing recipients to click on links or download attachments. Once opened, these emails can deliver viruses to the victim's system.

- **Malicious Attachments**: Viruses often hide within email attachments, including PDFs, Word documents, or compressed files. When opened, these attachments execute the virus.

- **Drive-By Downloads**: Some emails contain links to malicious websites. Clicking on these links can trigger drive-by downloads, where malware is automatically downloaded and executed without user consent.

- **Spear Phishing**: Targeted attacks, known as spear phishing, tailor emails to specific individuals or organizations. These emails may use personalized information to increase the likelihood of infection.

2. Downloads: The Temptation of Free Software and Media

Downloads from the internet, including software, media, and documents, present another significant infection vector:

- **Malicious Websites**: Cybercriminals create fake or compromised websites that distribute infected files. Users may inadvertently download viruses while seeking legitimate content.

- **Freeware and Torrents**: Users often download cracked software, torrents, or pirated media from untrusted sources. These files can be vehicles for malware, as cybercriminals exploit the allure of free content.

- **Software Vulnerabilities**: Some viruses exploit vulnerabilities in software or web browsers, enabling drive-by downloads when users visit compromised or malicious websites.

- **Malvertising**: Malicious advertisements (malvertising) on legitimate websites can lead to the unintentional download and execution of malware when users click on the ads.

3. USB Drives: The Portable Menace

USB drives and other removable media are common infection vectors, particularly in corporate environments:

- **AutoRun and AutoPlay**: Viruses can take advantage of AutoRun and AutoPlay features in operating systems, automatically executing when a USB drive is plugged in.

- **File Sharing**: When users share USB drives, they can unknowingly transmit viruses to other systems.

- **Lost and Found**: Users who find misplaced USB drives may plug them into their computers, unwittingly introducing malware to their systems.

- **Corporate Networks**: USB drives introduced into corporate networks can spread viruses rapidly, as malware can move between connected systems.

Understanding these infection vectors is vital for cybersecurity professionals and individuals alike. It empowers them to recognize potential threats, exercise caution when interacting with digital content, and employ security measures to defend against the relentless efforts of computer viruses to infiltrate and compromise systems.

B. Social Engineering and Phishing Attacks: Manipulating the Human Element

In the realm of cybersecurity, social engineering and phishing attacks represent a formidable threat, as they capitalize on human psychology and behavior to gain unauthorized access or extract sensitive information. These tactics rely on manipulation, deception, and the exploitation of trust, making them a potent vector for cybercriminals. In this comprehensive exploration, we delve into the intricate world of social engineering and phishing attacks, understanding their mechanisms, techniques, and countermeasures.

1. Social Engineering: The Art of Psychological Manipulation

Social engineering is a broad term that encompasses a range of techniques used to manipulate individuals into divulging confidential information, providing access, or performing specific actions. Here's an in-depth look at social engineering:

- **Pretexting**: This involves creating a fabricated scenario or pretext to trick individuals into disclosing sensitive information. For example, a pretexter might pose as an IT technician and request login credentials to "resolve a technical issue."

- **Phishing**: While phishing is commonly associated with email attacks, it's a broader social engineering technique. It involves using deceptive messages to trick recipients into revealing personal information, such as usernames, passwords, or financial details.

- **Baiting**: Baiting lures victims into taking specific actions by offering something appealing, such as a free download. Once the victim takes the bait, malware is often delivered.

- **Quid Pro Quo**: Attackers promise something in return for information or access. For instance, they may claim to be from a research organization and offer a reward in exchange for survey participation, which includes revealing sensitive data.

2. Phishing Attacks: The Deceptive Art of Impersonation

Phishing attacks are a prevalent form of social engineering, characterized by deceptive messages and impersonation. Here's an in-depth look at phishing attacks:

- **Email Phishing**: Phishing emails often appear legitimate, mimicking trusted entities like banks, government agencies, or well-known companies. They typically contain a call to action, such as clicking a link or opening an attachment.

- **Spear Phishing**: Spear phishing targets specific individuals or organizations, tailoring the attack to exploit personal information or organizational relationships. Attackers often research their targets extensively to craft convincing messages.

- **Whaling**: This form of phishing specifically targets high-profile individuals, such as executives or celebrities. The goal is to gain access to their accounts or extract sensitive information.

- **Smishing**: Smishing, or SMS phishing, employs text messages to deceive victims. These messages may contain links to malicious websites or instruct recipients to reply with sensitive information.

3. Techniques and Red Flags

Recognizing social engineering and phishing attacks requires an understanding of common techniques and red flags:

- **Urgency and Fear**: Attackers often create a sense of urgency or fear in their messages to pressure victims into immediate action.

- **Unsolicited Requests**: Unsolicited emails or messages requesting sensitive information should raise suspicion. Verify the sender's identity independently.

- **Misspelled URLs and Email Addresses**: Carefully inspect URLs and email addresses for misspellings or variations that resemble legitimate domains.

- **Attachments and Downloads**: Exercise caution when opening attachments or downloading files, especially from unknown sources.

4. Countermeasures and Security Awareness

Mitigating social engineering and phishing attacks requires a multi-pronged approach:

- **Security Awareness Training**: Educate users about the tactics used in social engineering and phishing attacks, emphasizing the importance of skepticism and verifying requests for sensitive information.

- **Email Filtering**: Implement email filtering solutions that can detect and quarantine phishing emails.

- **Two-Factor Authentication (2FA)**: Encourage the use of 2FA to add an extra layer of security, even if login credentials are compromised.

- **Regular Updates**: Ensure that systems and software are regularly updated with security patches to prevent known vulnerabilities from being exploited.

- **Incident Response Plans**: Develop incident response plans to swiftly address and contain security breaches when they occur.

Social engineering and phishing attacks remain a pervasive threat, emphasizing the critical role of security awareness and proactive defense measures in safeguarding individuals and organizations against the manipulative tactics employed by cybercriminals.

C. Drive-By Downloads and Malvertisements: The Silent Threats of the Web

In the ever-evolving landscape of cybersecurity, drive-by downloads and malvertisements stand out as stealthy and malicious tactics used by cybercriminals to compromise systems and steal sensitive information. These threats capitalize on users' trust in websites and online content, making them challenging to detect and defend against. In this comprehensive exploration, we delve into the intricate world of drive-by downloads and malvertisements, understanding their mechanisms, risks, and preventive measures.

1. Drive-By Downloads: The Uninvited Guests

Drive-by downloads are a category of web-based attacks where malware is automatically and often silently downloaded to a user's device without their consent or knowledge. Here's an in-depth look at drive-by downloads:

- **Exploiting Vulnerabilities**: Drive-by downloads often exploit vulnerabilities in web browsers, browser extensions, or plugins. When a user visits a compromised or malicious website, the malware leverages these vulnerabilities to initiate the download.

- **No User Interaction**: Unlike traditional downloads, where users intentionally click on a link or download button, drive-by downloads occur without any user interaction or consent. Victims may not even be aware that malware has been downloaded to their device.

- **Payload Variety**: The downloaded malware can vary

widely, from Trojans and ransomware to spyware and rootkits. The specific payload depends on the attacker's objectives.

• **Mitigation Challenges**: Detecting and mitigating drive-by downloads can be challenging, as they often occur on legitimate websites that have been compromised.

2. Malvertisements: Advertising Gone Rogue

Malvertisements, short for malicious advertisements, are online advertisements that carry hidden malware or lead users to malicious websites. Here's an in-depth look at malvertisements:

• **Distribution through Ad Networks**: Malvertisements are typically distributed through online advertising networks. Cybercriminals infiltrate these networks to inject malicious code into legitimate ad content.

• **Exploiting Trust**: Malvertisements often appear on reputable websites, exploiting the trust users have in these platforms. Users may click on the ads, assuming they are safe.

• **Payload Delivery**: Malvertisements can deliver various payloads, including exploit kits that target known vulnerabilities in web browsers or plugins. These payloads can lead to drive-by downloads when users interact with the ad.

• **Mobile Threat**: Malvertisements are not limited to desktops; they also target mobile devices through mobile apps and websites.

3. Risks and Impact

Drive-by downloads and malvertisements pose significant risks to users and organizations:

- **Data Theft**: Malware delivered through these methods can steal sensitive information, such as login credentials, financial data, or personal information.

- **System Compromise**: Drive-by downloads can compromise the integrity of a user's device, potentially leading to unauthorized access or control by attackers.

- **Financial Loss**: Malvertisements may lead to fraudulent websites that attempt to steal payment information or engage in financial scams.

- **Reputation Damage**: For organizations, hosting malvertisements or being a victim of drive-by downloads can damage their reputation and erode user trust.

4. Preventive Measures

Mitigating drive-by downloads and malvertisements requires proactive security measures:

- **Regular Software Updates**: Keep web browsers, plugins, and operating systems up-to-date to patch known vulnerabilities.

- **Ad Blockers**: Use ad-blocking browser extensions or software to reduce the risk of encountering malvertisements.

- **Web Filtering**: Employ web filtering solutions that block access to known malicious websites and ad networks.

- **Security Awareness**: Educate users about the risks of drive-by downloads and malvertisements, emphasizing the importance of cautious online behavior.

- **Endpoint Security**: Implement endpoint security solutions that can detect and prevent malware from executing on users' devices.

Drive-by downloads and malvertisements represent a silent yet potent threat in the digital landscape. Staying informed, exercising caution when encountering online ads or visiting websites, and maintaining up-to-date security measures are crucial steps in defending against these insidious cyberattacks.

D. Malware Distribution Networks: The Underground Infrastructure of Cybercrime

Behind every successful malware attack lies a complex web of infrastructure responsible for distributing malicious software to unsuspecting victims. These networks, often hidden in the depths of the dark web, facilitate the propagation of malware on a global scale. In this comprehensive exploration, we delve into the intricate world of malware distribution networks, understanding their structure, mechanisms, and the challenges they pose to cybersecurity.

1. Structure of Malware Distribution Networks

Malware distribution networks are comprised of various elements and actors working together to achieve their objectives:

• **Malware Authors**: These individuals or groups are responsible for developing and creating the malicious software that will be distributed. They may specialize in crafting specific types of malware, such as ransomware or banking Trojans.

• **Exploit Developers**: Exploits are tools or code that target vulnerabilities in software or systems. Exploit developers create and sell these tools, which malware authors use to infiltrate systems.

• **Botnet Operators**: Botnets are networks of infected computers, or "bots," controlled by a central server. Botnet operators manage these networks and use them for various malicious activities, including malware distribution.

• **Infrastructure Providers**: Hosting providers, domain registrars, and anonymous web hosting services may unknowingly or knowingly host malicious websites, serving as crucial components of malware distribution networks.

- **Payment Processors**: Cybercriminals rely on payment processors to receive payments for their services, such as selling malware or hosting malicious content.

2. Mechanisms of Malware Distribution

Malware distribution networks employ a variety of mechanisms to disseminate malicious software:

- **Drive-By Downloads**: As discussed previously, drive-by downloads occur when a victim visits a compromised or malicious website, which then exploits vulnerabilities in their system to deliver malware.

- **Phishing Emails**: Phishing emails distributed through spam campaigns can contain malicious attachments or links to malware-infected websites.

- **Malvertisements**: Malvertisements, distributed through legitimate ad networks, can lead users to websites hosting exploit kits that deliver malware.

- **File Sharing and Torrents**: Cybercriminals may upload infected files to popular file-sharing platforms or torrents, luring users into downloading malware-laden content.

- **Social Engineering**: Malware distribution networks often exploit social engineering tactics to deceive users into taking actions that lead to malware infections.

3. Dark Web Marketplaces

The dark web plays a significant role in facilitating malware distribution networks. Underground marketplaces on the dark web offer a range of illicit services, including the sale of malware, exploit kits, and compromised data. These marketplaces provide anonymity to cybercriminals and serve as hubs for the exchange of malicious tools and services.

4. Evolving Threat Landscape

Malware distribution networks continually adapt to evade detection and mitigation efforts:

- **Fast Flux Hosting**: Some networks use fast flux hosting, a technique that rapidly changes the IP addresses associated with malicious websites, making it challenging to block or trace.

- **Bulletproof Hosting**: Cybercriminals may seek out bulletproof hosting services that prioritize anonymity and ignore abuse reports from law enforcement and security organizations.

- **Encryption and Evasion**: Malware authors employ encryption and obfuscation techniques to make their code difficult to analyze, allowing malware to bypass security measures.

5. Defense and Mitigation

Defending against malware distribution networks requires a multi-faceted approach:

- **Threat Intelligence**: Continuously monitor threat intelligence sources to stay informed about emerging threats and trends in malware distribution.

- **Network Security**: Implement robust network security measures, such as intrusion detection systems (IDS) and intrusion prevention systems (IPS), to detect and block malicious traffic.

- **User Education**: Educate users about the risks of downloading files or clicking on links from untrusted sources, and encourage cautious online behavior.

- **Security Software**: Use up-to-date antivirus and antimalware solutions that can detect and remove malicious software.

- **Law Enforcement**: Collaborate with law enforcement agencies to identify and take down malicious infrastructure and apprehend cybercriminals.

Malware distribution networks represent a critical aspect of the cyber threat landscape. Cybersecurity professionals must remain vigilant, adapt to emerging threats, and collaborate with law enforcement and other stakeholders to disrupt and dismantle these underground infrastructures that enable cybercrime on a global scale.

E. Zero-Day Exploits: The Unseen Threats Lurking in the Shadows

Zero-day exploits are among the most elusive and potent threats in the cybersecurity landscape. These attacks target vulnerabilities in software or hardware that are unknown to the vendor or unpatched at the time of the attack. As a result, they leave no opportunity for mitigation before exploitation. In this comprehensive exploration, we delve into the intricate world of zero-day exploits, understanding their significance, mechanics, and the challenges they pose to cybersecurity.

1. Understanding Zero-Day Exploits

Zero-day exploits derive their name from the fact that they take advantage of vulnerabilities that are "zero days old." This means that neither the software vendor nor the cybersecurity community is aware of the flaw, leaving no time for mitigation or patch development. Here's an in-depth look at these exploits:

- **Vulnerability Discovery**: Zero-day vulnerabilities are

often discovered by security researchers, but they can also be found by cybercriminals or state-sponsored threat actors. These vulnerabilities may exist in operating systems, software applications, web browsers, or even hardware components.

• **Silent Threat**: Zero-day exploits operate silently and covertly. They do not trigger alerts or raise suspicion until after the attack has occurred.

• **Target Variety**: Zero-day exploits can target a wide range of systems, including desktops, servers, mobile devices, and IoT devices. Any software or hardware with a vulnerability is potentially at risk.

2. Attack Process

The process of executing a zero-day exploit is intricate and typically follows these steps:

• **Vulnerability Discovery**: The attacker or researcher identifies a previously unknown vulnerability in a software or hardware product. This vulnerability is often referred to as the "zero-day."

• **Exploit Development**: The attacker crafts a malicious program or code, known as an exploit, to take advantage of the vulnerability. This code enables unauthorized access, privilege escalation, or other malicious actions.

- **Target Selection**: The attacker selects specific targets or systems they want to compromise. These targets may be individuals, organizations, or even critical infrastructure.

- **Delivery**: The exploit is delivered to the target system through various means, such as email attachments, malicious websites, or compromised software updates.

- **Execution**: Once the exploit is executed on the target system, it leverages the zero-day vulnerability to achieve its objective, which may include gaining access, stealing data, or infecting the system with malware.

- **Covering Tracks**: To maintain stealth and persistence, the attacker may take steps to cover their tracks, such as erasing logs or employing anti-forensic techniques.

3. Significance and Impact

Zero-day exploits have profound implications for cybersecurity:

- **Limited Defense**: Since zero-day vulnerabilities are unknown to vendors and security experts, there are no patches or mitigations available. This leaves affected systems highly vulnerable.

- **High-Value Targets**: Zero-day exploits are often used against high-value targets, such as government agencies, corporations, or critical infrastructure, where the potential rewards justify the risk.

- **Economic Consequences**: Zero-day exploits can lead to economic losses through data breaches, system disruptions, and the cost of incident response and recovery.

4. Mitigation and Defense

Mitigating the risks associated with zero-day exploits requires a proactive and multi-layered approach:

- **Vulnerability Management**: Implement a robust vulnerability management program to identify, assess, and remediate vulnerabilities as quickly as possible.

- **Network Monitoring**: Employ advanced network monitoring and intrusion detection systems to detect suspicious activity and anomalous behavior.

- **User Education**: Train users to recognize phishing attempts and other social engineering tactics that can be used to deliver zero-day exploits.

- **Behavioral Analytics**: Utilize behavioral analytics and machine learning to detect abnormal user or system behavior that may indicate a zero-day exploit.

- **Threat Intelligence**: Stay informed about emerging

threats and zero-day vulnerabilities by monitoring threat intelligence feeds and information-sharing networks.

Zero-day exploits remain a formidable challenge in the world of cybersecurity, highlighting the need for proactive defense strategies, timely patch management, and collaboration among security experts to discover and mitigate these threats before they can cause harm.

Chapter 4

Advanced Malware Analysis

In the relentless arms race between cybercriminals and cybersecurity experts, advanced malware analysis stands as a crucial bastion of defense. This chapter delves into the intricate art of dissecting and understanding the inner workings of sophisticated malware, equipping readers with the knowledge and techniques required to unravel its complexities, identify vulnerabilities, and fortify digital defenses against the ever-evolving threat landscape.

A. Behavioral Analysis of Malware: Unmasking Digital Adversaries

In the perpetual battle against cyber threats, understanding the behavior of malware is paramount. Behavioral analysis is a fundamental technique that allows cybersecurity experts to dissect and comprehend the actions and intentions of malicious software. By observing how malware behaves within a controlled environment, analysts can uncover its capabilities, objectives, and potential damage. In this in-depth exploration, we delve into the world of behavioral analysis of malware, revealing the tools, methodologies, and significance of this critical cybersecurity practice.

1. The Essence of Behavioral Analysis

Behavioral analysis involves studying how malware behaves when executed in a controlled environment. Instead of solely relying on static code analysis, which examines the code's characteristics without execution, behavioral analysis focuses on the dynamic actions of the malware as it runs. Here's an in-depth look at this technique:

- **Execution in a Sandbox**: Malware is executed within a controlled environment known as a sandbox or virtual machine. This environment isolates the malware from the host system, preventing it from causing harm.

- **Monitoring and Recording**: During execution, every action taken by the malware is meticulously monitored and recorded. This includes system interactions, file modifications, network traffic, and registry changes.

- **Behavioral Indicators**: Analysts pay close attention to behavioral indicators, such as system calls, API interactions, and patterns of activity. These indicators provide insights into the malware's functionality.

2. Significance of Behavioral Analysis

Behavioral analysis is invaluable for several reasons:

- **Uncovering Hidden Functionality**: Some malware conceals its true intentions until triggered by specific conditions or events. Behavioral analysis can reveal hidden functionality, shedding light on potential threats.

- **Customized Defense**: Understanding how malware behaves allows security experts to tailor defenses. They can develop signatures for intrusion detection systems, create YARA rules for identifying similar malware, or adjust security policies.

- **Zero-Day Detection**: Behavioral analysis is particularly effective in detecting zero-day exploits and previously unknown threats. By observing unusual behavior, analysts can identify emerging threats that lack signatures or known indicators.

3. Methodologies and Tools

Behavioral analysis employs various methodologies and tools:

- **Sandbox Environments**: Sandboxes, such as Cuckoo or FireEye, provide controlled environments for executing malware. They record behavioral data for analysis.

- **Dynamic Analysis**: Analysts perform dynamic analysis by executing malware samples and observing their behavior. This includes tracking system calls, file operations, and network traffic.

- **Static Analysis Complement**: Behavioral analysis

often complements static analysis. Static analysis examines the code without execution, providing information about code structure and potential vulnerabilities.

• **Traffic Analysis**: For malware that communicates over the network, monitoring network traffic is essential. Tools like Wireshark help capture and analyze this communication.

4. Challenges and Limitations

Behavioral analysis, while powerful, has its challenges:

• **Evasion Techniques**: Some advanced malware can detect sandbox environments and alter their behavior to evade analysis.

• **Resource Intensive**: Behavioral analysis can be resource-intensive, especially for large-scale operations or when dealing with complex malware.

• **Data Overload**: The volume of data generated during analysis can be overwhelming. Analysts must filter and prioritize relevant information.

5. Real-World Applications

Behavioral analysis is crucial in incident response, threat hunting, and malware research. It helps organizations identify and respond to security breaches, assess the impact of malware infections, and develop strategies to enhance cybersecurity posture.

In the ever-evolving landscape of cyber threats, behavioral analysis remains a vital tool for cybersecurity experts. It equips them with the means to dissect, understand, and combat malware effectively, making it an indispensable practice in safeguarding digital assets and data against the relentless tide of digital adversaries.

B. Signature-Based Detection: The Time-Tested Guardian of Cybersecurity

In the ongoing battle against malware and cyber threats, signature-based detection stands as one of the most established and effective defensive mechanisms. This approach relies on the identification of unique patterns, or "signatures," within the code or behavior of known malicious entities. By comparing incoming data or files to these signatures, security systems can swiftly identify and neutralize threats that match known attack patterns. In this in-depth exploration, we delve into the world of signature-based detection, understanding its principles, benefits, and the evolving challenges it faces in the ever-changing cybersecurity landscape.

1. The Fundamentals of Signature-Based Detection

Signature-based detection operates on the principle of recognizing the unique characteristics or patterns exhibited by known malware or cyber threats. Here's an in-depth look at the core principles of this approach:

- **Signature Creation**: Cybersecurity experts or threat intelligence teams create signatures by analyzing the code or behavior of known malicious software. These signatures often consist of specific sequences of bytes, file hashes, or behavioral patterns that are unique to the malware.

- **Pattern Matching**: When incoming data, files, or network traffic is examined, the security system scans for patterns that match known signatures. If a match is detected, it signifies a potential threat.

- **Rapid Response**: Signature-based detection enables rapid response to threats. Once a match is identified, the security system can trigger predefined actions, such as blocking, quarantining, or alerting administrators.

2. Benefits and Advantages

Signature-based detection offers several advantages:

- **Accuracy**: When faced with known threats, signature-based detection is highly accurate and rarely produces false positives.

- **Speed**: The process of matching incoming data against known signatures is fast, allowing for swift threat identification and response.

- **Proven Effectiveness**: Signature-based detection has a track record of effectively thwarting known malware and attacks, making it a reliable defense mechanism.

3. Limitations and Challenges

While effective, signature-based detection has notable limitations:

- **Limited to Known Threats**: This approach is only effective against threats with known signatures. Zero-day exploits and new, previously unseen malware often go undetected.

- **Maintenance Overhead**: Maintaining an up-to-date signature database requires constant effort. Security teams must regularly update signatures to remain effective against evolving threats.

- **False Negatives**: If malware authors modify their code slightly or employ evasion techniques, signature-based detection may fail to recognize the threat.

4. Real-World Applications

Signature-based detection is widely used in various cybersecurity applications:

- **Antivirus Software**: Antivirus solutions rely on signature databases to detect and quarantine known malware.

- **Intrusion Detection and Prevention Systems (IDPS)**: IDPS solutions use signatures to identify and block known attack patterns or malicious network traffic.

- **Email Filtering**: Email security systems employ signature-based detection to identify and filter out known phishing emails and malicious attachments.

- **Web Application Firewalls (WAFs)**: WAFs use signatures to identify and block known web-based attacks, such as SQL injection or cross-site scripting (XSS).

5. The Role in a Comprehensive Defense Strategy

While signature-based detection is a crucial component of cybersecurity, it is most effective when used in conjunction with other security measures. Modern defense strategies often incorporate behavioral analysis, machine learning, and heuristic techniques to detect threats beyond the scope of traditional signatures.

In the ever-evolving landscape of cyber threats, signature-based detection remains a stalwart guardian against known malicious entities. Its accuracy and speed make it an indispensable tool for identifying and mitigating threats with established patterns. However, to address the evolving challenges posed by new and sophisticated threats, organizations must adopt a multi-layered security approach that combines signature-based detection with other advanced techniques to ensure comprehensive protection against the ever-changing threat landscape.

C. Heuristics and Sandbox Analysis: Unmasking Hidden Threats

In the relentless pursuit of effective cybersecurity, heuristics and sandbox analysis have emerged as indispensable tools for identifying and mitigating advanced threats. These techniques are designed to uncover malicious software and vulnerabilities by examining patterns, behaviors, and attributes that may not be explicitly known or recognized. In this in-depth exploration, we delve into the realms of heuristics and sandbox analysis, unveiling their significance, methodologies, and how they contribute to fortifying digital defenses in the dynamic world of cyber threats.

1. Heuristics: A Proactive Approach to Threat Detection

Heuristics, in the context of cybersecurity, is a technique that focuses on identifying potential threats based on general characteristics and behaviors, rather than relying on specific signatures or known patterns. Here's an in-depth look at the principles and methodologies of heuristics:

- **Pattern Recognition**: Heuristics involves the analysis of data, files, or code to identify patterns or behaviors that are indicative of malicious intent. This may include suspicious code structures, obfuscation techniques, or unexpected data flows.

- **Proactive Approach**: Unlike signature-based detection, which relies on known patterns, heuristics take a proactive approach by identifying threats based on their characteristics, even if they have never been encountered before.

- **Anomaly Detection**: Heuristic systems often employ anomaly detection algorithms to flag deviations from expected behavior. Unusual activities or patterns can trigger alerts or further analysis.

- **Machine Learning**: Machine learning models are increasingly integrated into heuristic systems, enabling them to learn and adapt to evolving threats over time.

2. Sandbox Analysis: Testing in a Controlled Environment

Sandbox analysis is a technique that involves executing potentially malicious code or software in an isolated and controlled environment, known as a sandbox. The primary objective is to observe the behavior of the code without risking harm to the host system. Here's an in-depth look at the principles and methodologies of sandbox analysis:

- **Controlled Environment**: Sandboxes provide a safe and controlled environment where code can be executed, monitored, and analyzed. This isolation prevents malware from causing harm to the host system.

- **Behavioral Analysis**: During sandbox analysis, the behavior of the code is closely monitored. This includes interactions with the file system, registry, network, and other system resources.

- **Traffic Analysis**: Network traffic generated by the code is captured and analyzed to determine whether the code attempts to communicate with malicious servers or engage in other suspicious activities.

- **Dynamic Analysis**: Sandbox analysis is dynamic, meaning it observes how the code behaves in real-time, allowing for the detection of actions that may not be apparent from static analysis alone.

3. Significance and Applications

Heuristics and sandbox analysis are crucial components of modern cybersecurity:

- **Advanced Threat Detection**: Heuristics and sandbox analysis are effective in identifying advanced threats, including zero-day exploits and malware with polymorphic or obfuscated code.

- **Zero-Day Protection**: These techniques can detect and mitigate threats that lack known signatures or patterns, making them valuable for zero-day protection.

- **Behavioral Insights**: Heuristics and sandbox analysis provide insights into the behavior and intentions of threats, helping security experts understand the scope of an attack and its potential impact.

4. Limitations and Challenges

While heuristics and sandbox analysis are powerful, they are not without limitations:

- **False Positives**: Heuristic systems may generate false positives if legitimate software exhibits behavior that is similar to malicious code.

- **Evasion Techniques**: Sophisticated malware may employ evasion techniques to avoid detection in sandbox environments.

- **Resource Intensive**: Sandboxing can be resource-intensive, especially when analyzing large or complex files or code.

5. The Role in a Comprehensive Defense Strategy

Heuristics and sandbox analysis are integral components of a comprehensive cybersecurity strategy. They complement signature-based detection and other security measures by offering proactive threat detection capabilities. To address the evolving threat landscape, organizations often combine these techniques with behavioral analysis, machine learning, and threat intelligence to build resilient and adaptive defenses against cyber threats.

D. Machine Learning in Malware Detection: Unleashing Artificial Intelligence Against Cyber Threats

In the ever-evolving landscape of cybersecurity, machine learning has emerged as a formidable ally in the battle against malware and other digital threats. Machine learning leverages algorithms and data to train models that can identify, classify, and even predict malicious activity. In this in-depth exploration, we delve into the world of machine learning in malware detection, understanding its principles, applications, and the pivotal role it plays in fortifying digital defenses in the face of evolving cyber threats.

1. Machine Learning Fundamentals

Machine learning, a subset of artificial intelligence (AI), focuses on developing algorithms and models that can learn from data and make predictions or decisions without explicit programming. In the context of cybersecurity and malware detection, machine learning is applied to identify patterns and anomalies indicative of malicious behavior. Here's an in-depth look at the fundamentals:

- **Training Data**: Machine learning models are trained using labeled datasets that include examples of both benign and malicious software. The model learns to distinguish between the two based on features extracted from the data.

- **Feature Engineering**: Features are characteristics or attributes extracted from data samples. In malware detection, features may include code patterns, file attributes, API calls, and more. Effective feature engineering is crucial for model accuracy.

- **Supervised and Unsupervised Learning**: Supervised learning involves training models with labeled data, while unsupervised learning identifies patterns in data without predefined labels. Both approaches are used in malware detection.

2. Machine Learning Applications in Malware Detection

Machine learning has a wide range of applications in malware detection:

- **Malware Classification**: Machine learning models can classify files or code as benign or malicious. This classification can be based on static analysis (examining file attributes) or dynamic analysis (observing behavior).

- **Anomaly Detection**: Unsupervised learning models can identify anomalies in system behavior that may indicate a malware infection. This approach is valuable for detecting zero-day threats.

- **Threat Intelligence**: Machine learning can be used to analyze vast amounts of threat intelligence data, identifying emerging threats and trends that may go unnoticed by human analysts.

- **Email Security**: Machine learning is employed in email security solutions to detect phishing emails, malicious attachments, and spam.

3. Types of Machine Learning Models

Several types of machine learning models are applied in malware detection:

- **Decision Trees**: Decision tree models use a hierarchical structure of decisions and outcomes to classify data.

- **Random Forest**: Random forests are ensembles of decision trees, providing enhanced accuracy and robustness.

- **Support Vector Machines (SVM)**: SVM models find the hyperplane that best separates data points, making them effective for binary classification tasks.

- **Neural Networks**: Deep learning models, such as convolutional neural networks (CNNs) and recurrent neural networks (RNNs), have demonstrated exceptional performance in image-based malware detection and sequence-based analysis.

- **Clustering Algorithms**: Unsupervised learning models like k-means clustering can identify clusters of similar data points, which may include malware samples.

4. Real-World Significance

Machine learning in malware detection offers several advantages:

- **Adaptability**: Machine learning models can adapt to new threats and evolving attack techniques, making them highly relevant in the face of constantly changing malware.

- **Scalability**: Machine learning can analyze large datasets and automate the analysis process, enabling efficient handling of massive amounts of data.

- **Speed**: Machine learning algorithms can process data quickly, allowing for near-real-time threat detection and response.

5. Challenges and Considerations

Machine learning in malware detection is not without challenges:

- **Adversarial Attacks**: Malicious actors can attempt to manipulate or evade machine learning models, posing a challenge for robustness.

- **Data Privacy**: Handling sensitive data for model training raises privacy and security concerns.

- **False Positives and Negatives**: Achieving the right balance between false positives and false negatives is crucial to minimize both missed threats and unnecessary alerts.

6. The Role in a Comprehensive Defense Strategy

Machine learning is a cornerstone of modern cybersecurity strategies. When combined with other techniques such as signature-based detection, behavioral analysis, and threat intelligence, it enhances an organization's ability to identify and mitigate a broad spectrum of cyber threats. As malware becomes more sophisticated, machine learning continues to evolve and play a pivotal role in staying one step ahead of cyber adversaries.

E. Reverse Engineering Malware: Decrypting the Digital Threats

In the relentless battle against cyber threats, reverse engineering malware stands as a crucial and intricate process for dissecting, understanding, and neutralizing malicious software. Cybersecurity experts employ reverse engineering to unveil the inner workings of malware, analyze its behavior, and develop countermeasures. In this comprehensive exploration, we delve into the world of reverse engineering malware, uncovering its significance, methodologies, and the pivotal role it plays in fortifying digital defenses against evolving cyber threats.

1. The Essence of Reverse Engineering Malware

Reverse engineering malware is a process that involves taking apart malicious software to gain insights into its functionality, code structure, and intent. This practice is essential for understanding how malware operates, identifying vulnerabilities, and developing effective defenses. Here's an in-depth look at the principles and methodologies of reverse engineering malware:

- **Objectives**: The primary objectives of reverse engineering malware include understanding its behavior, uncovering its command and control mechanisms, identifying evasion techniques, and discovering any potential vulnerabilities or exploits.

- **Code Analysis**: Analysts examine the binary code of

malware to understand its functions, algorithms, and execution flow. This often involves disassembling or decompiling the code into a human-readable format.

- **Behavioral Analysis**: Beyond code analysis, reverse engineering involves observing how the malware behaves when executed in a controlled environment, such as a sandbox. This helps uncover hidden functionality and interactions with the host system.

- **Reconstruction**: In some cases, reverse engineering may involve reconstructing the source code or creating a higher-level representation of the malware to facilitate analysis and mitigation.

2. The Significance of Reverse Engineering

Reverse engineering malware holds immense significance in the field of cybersecurity:

- **Threat Understanding**: By reverse engineering malware, cybersecurity experts gain a deeper understanding of the threats they face, including their capabilities, propagation methods, and objectives.

- **Vulnerability Identification**: Reverse engineering can uncover vulnerabilities within the malware itself, allowing for the development of patches or mitigations to protect against its exploitation.

- **Mitigation Development**: Insights gained from reverse engineering enable the development of defensive measures, such as antivirus signatures, intrusion detection rules, and security patches.

- **Attribution**: In some cases, reverse engineering may help attribute the malware to specific threat actors or cybercriminal groups, aiding in investigations.

3. Methodologies and Tools

Reverse engineering malware requires a combination of methodologies and tools:

- **Disassemblers and Decompilers**: Tools like IDA Pro, Ghidra, and Binary Ninja assist in disassembling and decompiling binary code into human-readable formats.

- **Dynamic Analysis**: Sandboxes and virtual environments allow analysts to execute malware in a controlled setting and monitor its behavior.

- **Memory Analysis**: Memory analysis tools like Volatility help extract valuable information from a running malware process.

- **Debugger and Debugging Tools**: Debuggers like

OllyDbg and WinDbg enable analysts to step through code, set breakpoints, and examine registers and memory.

• **Static Analysis Tools**: Static analysis tools can automatically analyze binary code to identify known patterns and behaviors.

4. Challenges and Expertise

Reverse engineering malware is not without challenges:

• **Code Obfuscation**: Malware authors often employ code obfuscation techniques to make analysis more challenging.

• **Evasion Techniques**: Sophisticated malware may employ anti-analysis and evasion techniques to detect the presence of a sandbox or debugger.

• **Complexity**: Some malware is highly complex, requiring significant expertise and time to reverse engineer effectively.

5. Legal and Ethical Considerations

Reverse engineering malware must be conducted within legal and ethical boundaries. Unauthorized reverse engineering may violate laws and regulations, and analysts must adhere to ethical guidelines in handling malware samples.

6. The Role in a Comprehensive Defense Strategy

Reverse engineering malware is an integral component of a comprehensive defense strategy. It empowers organizations to understand and respond effectively to cyber threats. By dissecting and demystifying malicious software, cybersecurity experts can develop tailored defenses, share threat intelligence, and contribute to the ongoing battle against cyber adversaries. As malware continues to evolve, reverse engineering remains a pivotal practice in staying one step ahead of digital threats.

Chapter 5

Antivirus Technologies and Strategies

In the ever-expanding digital landscape, where cyber threats are continually evolving in sophistication and scale, antivirus technologies and strategies serve as the stalwart guardians of digital security. This chapter embarks on a comprehensive exploration of antivirus solutions, unveiling their principles, capabilities, and strategic implementations. From real-time scanning to heuristic analysis and cloud-based threat detection, we delve into the arsenal of tools and tactics employed by antivirus systems to shield individuals and organizations from the relentless onslaught of malware and cyber threats.

A. Antivirus Software Features: Shields Against the Digital Onslaught

Antivirus software has become a cornerstone of modern cybersecurity, providing a crucial layer of defense against the relentless tide of malware and cyber threats. These software solutions are equipped with a diverse range of features designed to detect, quarantine, and neutralize malicious software. In this in-depth exploration, we delve into the multifaceted world of antivirus software features, understanding their significance, capabilities, and the pivotal role they play in safeguarding digital assets and data from the ever-evolving threat landscape.

1. Real-Time Scanning

Real-time scanning is the foundation of antivirus software. It involves the continuous monitoring of files, programs, and system activities in real-time to identify and block malicious code or behavior. Here's an in-depth look at this fundamental feature:

- **File System Monitoring**: Antivirus software keeps a watchful eye on files as they are created, accessed, modified, or executed. Any suspicious activity or code triggers an alert or action.

- **Memory Scanning**: Real-time scanning extends to monitoring processes running in memory, identifying and terminating malicious processes.

- **Web Traffic Inspection**: Some antivirus solutions inspect web traffic in real-time, preventing users from visiting malicious websites or downloading infected files.

2. Behavioral Analysis

Behavioral analysis is a more advanced feature that goes beyond signature-based detection. It involves observing the behavior of files or processes to identify anomalies indicative of malware. Here's an in-depth look:

- **Heuristic Analysis**: Antivirus software employs heuristics to detect behaviors that may resemble those of known malware, even if no specific signature is present.

- **Sandboxing**: Some solutions execute potentially suspicious files or code in a controlled environment (sandbox) to observe their behavior without risking the host system.

- **Machine Learning**: Machine learning models can analyze behavior and identify patterns or anomalies, helping detect previously unknown threats.

3. Heuristic and Cloud-Based Detection

Heuristic analysis is a feature that identifies potential threats based on general characteristics and behavior, rather than specific signatures. Cloud-based detection extends this capability by leveraging the power of the cloud to analyze files and data. Here's an in-depth look:

- **Unknown Threats**: Heuristic analysis and cloud-based detection are particularly effective at identifying zero-day exploits and new, previously unseen malware.

- **Near-Instant Updates**: Cloud-based systems can rapidly update threat databases, ensuring that endpoints are protected against emerging threats.

- **Reduced Resource Usage**: Offloading some detection

processes to the cloud can reduce the system resource overhead on endpoints.

4. Advanced Threat Protection

Antivirus software often includes advanced threat protection features designed to defend against a wide range of sophisticated attacks:

- **Email Filtering**: Many antivirus solutions provide email filtering capabilities to detect and block phishing emails, malicious attachments, and spam.

- **Ransomware Protection**: Some solutions offer dedicated ransomware protection, which can identify and block ransomware attacks before they can encrypt files.

- **Intrusion Detection**: Intrusion detection capabilities can identify and respond to unauthorized access attempts or suspicious network traffic.

5. Evaluating Antivirus Solutions

When selecting antivirus software, it's essential to consider various factors, including:

- **Effectiveness**: Assess the software's ability to detect and block known threats as well as its effectiveness in identifying new and emerging threats.

- **Resource Usage**: Evaluate the impact of the antivirus software on system performance, as heavy resource usage can affect user experience.

- **Ease of Management**: Consider the ease of installation, configuration, and management, particularly for organizations with multiple endpoints.

- **Scalability**: Ensure the software can scale to accommodate the needs of your organization as it grows.

- **Updates and Support**: Regular updates and access to support services are critical for maintaining the software's effectiveness.

6. The Role in a Comprehensive Defense Strategy

Antivirus software features, when integrated into a broader cybersecurity strategy, play a pivotal role in safeguarding digital assets and data. By offering real-time scanning, behavioral analysis, heuristic detection, and advanced threat protection, antivirus solutions contribute to the ongoing battle against malware and cyber threats. However, to address the evolving threat landscape effectively, organizations often combine antivirus software with other security measures, such as firewalls, intrusion detection systems, and user education, to create a comprehensive defense strategy that fortifies the digital perimeter and safeguards against a diverse array of threats.

B. Real-Time Scanning and Behavioral Analysis: Vigilant Guardians of Digital Security

In the ever-evolving world of cybersecurity, real-time scanning and behavioral analysis are two integral components of modern antivirus and security solutions. These techniques are designed to detect and respond to threats swiftly, offering real-time protection against malware and other malicious activities. In this comprehensive exploration, we delve into the intricate workings of real-time scanning and behavioral analysis, understanding their significance, methodologies, and the pivotal roles they play in fortifying digital defenses against the relentless tide of cyber threats.

1. Real-Time Scanning: The First Line of Defense

Real-time scanning, also known as on-access scanning, is a foundational feature of antivirus and security software. It involves the continuous monitoring of files, programs, and system activities as they are accessed, created, modified, or executed. Here's an in-depth look at the principles and methodologies of real-time scanning:

- **File System Monitoring**: Antivirus software continuously watches over files within the file system. As files are accessed or executed, the software scans them for known malware signatures, patterns, or behaviors.

- **Memory Scanning**: Real-time scanning extends to monitoring processes running in computer memory (RAM). Any malicious processes detected are terminated promptly.

- **Web Traffic Inspection**: Some antivirus solutions include web traffic inspection, examining data flowing between the user's computer and the internet. Suspicious or potentially harmful content is blocked before it reaches the user's system.

- **Email Filtering**: Real-time scanning often integrates with email clients, inspecting incoming emails and attachments for malware, phishing attempts, and other threats.

2. Behavioral Analysis: Unmasking the Unseen Threats

Behavioral analysis, also known as behavior-based detection, takes a proactive approach to threat identification. Rather than relying solely on known signatures, this technique observes the behavior of files, processes, and activities to detect anomalies indicative of malware. Here's an in-depth look at the principles and methodologies of behavioral analysis:

- **Heuristic Analysis**: Antivirus software employs heuristics to identify behaviors that may resemble those of known malware, even if no specific signature is present. It looks for patterns of behavior that are consistent with malicious intent.

- **Sandboxing**: Some solutions execute potentially

suspicious files or code in a controlled environment called a sandbox. Here, the software observes how the code behaves, allowing it to identify hidden functionality, evasion tactics, and malicious interactions with the host system.

- **Machine Learning**: Machine learning models, trained on vast datasets of benign and malicious behaviors, analyze the behavior of files or processes to detect patterns or anomalies. These models can adapt and learn from new threats over time.

3. Significance and Applications

Real-time scanning and behavioral analysis offer several advantages:

- **Swift Threat Detection**: Real-time scanning provides immediate protection, identifying and blocking threats as they attempt to infiltrate the system.

- **Proactive Detection**: Behavioral analysis is proactive, capable of identifying new and previously unknown threats, including zero-day exploits and polymorphic malware.

- **Adaptability**: Machine learning models in behavioral analysis can adapt to evolving threats and learn to recognize new behaviors indicative of malicious intent.

4. Limitations and Challenges

While effective, these techniques have limitations:

• **False Positives**: Real-time scanning and behavioral analysis can generate false positives, flagging legitimate software as potentially malicious if it exhibits behavior that resembles malware.

• **Resource Usage**: Continuous real-time scanning can consume system resources and impact performance, although modern solutions aim to minimize this.

• **Evasion Techniques**: Advanced malware may employ evasion techniques to avoid detection, making it challenging for both real-time scanning and behavioral analysis to identify them.

5. The Role in a Comprehensive Defense Strategy

Real-time scanning and behavioral analysis, when integrated into a comprehensive defense strategy, serve as vigilant guardians of digital security. By offering immediate protection against known threats and proactive detection of emerging ones, these techniques contribute to the ongoing battle against malware and cyber threats. In today's dynamic threat landscape, organizations often combine these techniques with other security measures, such as signature-based detection, intrusion detection systems, and user education, to create a resilient and layered defense strategy that safeguards digital assets and data against a diverse array of threats.

C. Heuristics and Cloud-Based Detection: The Dynamic Duo in Modern Malware Defense

In the perpetual cat-and-mouse game of cybersecurity, heuristics and cloud-based detection are two formidable allies that play pivotal roles in identifying and mitigating malware threats. These techniques bring proactive and scalable approaches to the table, enabling security systems to combat evolving cyber threats effectively. In this in-depth exploration, we delve into the dynamic world of heuristics and cloud-based detection, understanding their significance, methodologies, and how they jointly strengthen the defenses against the ever-shifting landscape of malware.

1. Heuristics: Proactive Threat Recognition

Heuristics, as applied in the context of cybersecurity, refers to a proactive approach to identifying threats based on general characteristics and behavior, rather than relying solely on specific signatures or known patterns. Here's an in-depth look at the principles and methodologies of heuristics:

- **Pattern Recognition**: Heuristics involves the analysis of data, files, or code to identify patterns or behaviors that are indicative of malicious intent. This may include recognizing suspicious code structures, obfuscation techniques, or unexpected data flows.

• **Proactive Stance**: Unlike signature-based detection, which relies on known patterns, heuristics is proactive. It seeks to identify potential threats based on their characteristics, even if those threats have never been encountered before.

• **Anomaly Detection**: Heuristic systems often employ anomaly detection algorithms to flag deviations from expected behavior. Unusual activities or patterns can trigger alerts or further analysis.

• **Machine Learning**: Modern heuristics may integrate machine learning models to analyze and identify patterns or anomalies in real-time, allowing for the detection of previously unseen threats.

2. Cloud-Based Detection: Harnessing Collective Intelligence

Cloud-based detection extends the capabilities of antivirus and security solutions by leveraging the power of the cloud to analyze files, data, and network traffic. Here's an in-depth look at the principles and methodologies of cloud-based detection:

• **Real-Time Analysis**: Cloud-based detection systems can analyze incoming files and data in real-time. This includes scrutinizing attachments in emails, files downloaded from the internet, and more.

- **Collective Intelligence**: These systems tap into a collective pool of threat intelligence gathered from various sources, including multiple users and organizations. This intelligence helps identify emerging threats quickly.

- **Scalability**: Cloud-based systems can easily scale to accommodate the growing volumes of data and the evolving threat landscape. This scalability ensures that protection remains effective, even as the number and complexity of threats increase.

- **Rapid Updates**: Cloud-based systems can receive near-instant updates to threat databases, enabling endpoints to stay protected against emerging threats.

3. Significance and Applications

Heuristics and cloud-based detection offer several advantages:

- **Proactive Defense**: Heuristics proactively identifies potential threats based on behavior and characteristics, making it effective against zero-day exploits and new, previously unseen malware.

- **Scalable Protection**: Cloud-based detection scales effortlessly, providing effective protection for organizations of all sizes without imposing excessive resource usage on individual endpoints.

- **Rapid Threat Response**: Cloud-based systems offer near-instant updates and access to the latest threat intelligence, allowing for rapid threat detection and response.

4. Limitations and Challenges

While effective, these techniques have limitations:

- **False Positives**: Heuristic systems may generate false positives if legitimate software exhibits behavior that resembles malware.

- **Resource Usage**: Cloud-based detection may introduce latency if the network connection is slow, and it relies on cloud resources, which could be overwhelmed during massive cyberattacks.

- **Data Privacy**: Transmitting data to the cloud for analysis raises privacy concerns, particularly for sensitive information.

5. The Role in a Comprehensive Defense Strategy

Heuristics and cloud-based detection, when integrated into a comprehensive defense strategy, bolster an organization's ability to detect and mitigate a broad spectrum of cyber threats. By offering proactive threat recognition, scalability, and access to collective intelligence, these techniques contribute to the ongoing battle against malware and cyber adversaries. To address the evolving threat landscape effectively, organizations often combine heuristics and cloud-based detection with other security measures, such as real-time scanning, behavioral analysis, and user education, to create a multi-layered defense strategy that fortifies digital assets and data against a diverse array of threats.

D. Advanced Threat Protection: Fortifying Digital Defenses Against Sophisticated Adversaries

In the fast-paced and ever-evolving realm of cybersecurity, advanced threat protection emerges as a critical line of defense against increasingly sophisticated cyber adversaries. This comprehensive strategy encompasses a range of proactive and reactive measures designed to detect, mitigate, and thwart advanced threats. In this in-depth exploration, we delve into the world of advanced threat protection, understanding its significance, methodologies, and the pivotal role it plays in fortifying digital defenses against the relentless and evolving landscape of cyber threats.

1. The Significance of Advanced Threat Protection

Advanced threat protection has gained paramount importance due to several factors:

- **Sophistication of Threats**: Cyber adversaries

continually refine their tactics, techniques, and procedures (TTPs) to launch advanced attacks that evade traditional security measures.

- **Targeted Attacks**: Advanced threats often target specific organizations or individuals, making them challenging to detect using generic security solutions.

- **Financial Impact**: Successful advanced attacks can result in severe financial losses, reputational damage, and legal repercussions for organizations.

- **Data Protection**: The protection of sensitive data, intellectual property, and customer information is paramount in today's interconnected world.

2. Components of Advanced Threat Protection

Advanced threat protection encompasses a suite of components and strategies:

- **Advanced Malware Detection**: Solutions employ advanced techniques, such as heuristics, behavioral analysis, and machine learning, to detect malware that evades signature-based detection.

- **Sandboxing**: Sandboxes are controlled environments where suspicious files or code are executed to observe their behavior without risk to the host system.

- **Threat Intelligence**: Organizations rely on threat intelligence feeds and services to stay updated on the latest threat actors, tactics, and indicators of compromise (IOCs).

- **Security Analytics**: Advanced threat protection solutions often employ security analytics to identify anomalies in network traffic and user behavior.

- **Incident Response Plans**: Organizations develop and implement incident response plans and procedures to detect, contain, and remediate advanced threats.

3. Threat Vectors and Attack Techniques

Advanced threat protection covers various threat vectors and attack techniques, including:

- **Phishing**: Phishing attacks attempt to deceive users into revealing sensitive information or downloading malicious payloads through emails, social engineering, or other means.

- **Zero-Day Exploits**: Attackers target software vulnerabilities that have not been publicly disclosed or patched, making them challenging to defend against.

- **Advanced Persistent Threats (APTs)**: APTs involve stealthy and prolonged attacks by well-funded and organized threat actors with specific objectives.

- **Insider Threats**: Threats from within an organization can be challenging to detect, as insiders have legitimate access to systems and data.

- **Malware Evasion**: Malware authors employ evasion techniques like code obfuscation, polymorphism, and anti-analysis tactics to avoid detection.

4. Proactive Measures in Advanced Threat Protection

Proactive measures are essential in advanced threat protection:

- **Employee Education**: User training and awareness programs educate employees about potential threats, phishing, and safe online practices.

- **Access Control**: Implementing the principle of least privilege restricts user access to only the resources necessary for their roles.

- **Patch Management**: Timely application of security patches and updates helps eliminate known vulnerabilities.

- **Security Monitoring**: Continuous monitoring of network traffic and system logs helps identify suspicious activities and potential threats.

5. The Role of Automation and Artificial Intelligence

Automation and artificial intelligence (AI) are integral to

advanced threat protection:

- **Automated Threat Detection**: Automated systems can quickly detect and respond to threats, reducing the time to detection and containment.

- **Machine Learning**: Machine learning models can analyze vast amounts of data to identify patterns and anomalies indicative of advanced threats.

6. Limitations and Challenges

Despite its effectiveness, advanced threat protection faces challenges:

- **Resource Intensity**: Implementing and maintaining advanced threat protection solutions can be resource-intensive, requiring specialized skills and technology.

- **Evasion Tactics**: Advanced adversaries continuously develop new evasion tactics, necessitating ongoing innovation in threat protection.

- **False Positives**: Sophisticated solutions may generate false positives, leading to unnecessary alerts and potentially alert fatigue.

7. The Role in a Comprehensive Defense Strategy

Advanced threat protection is a cornerstone of a comprehensive cybersecurity strategy. By integrating advanced detection techniques, threat intelligence, incident response, and proactive measures, organizations can strengthen their defenses against the evolving threat landscape. While advanced threats continue to evolve, advanced threat protection remains an essential component in staying one step ahead of cyber adversaries, protecting valuable assets, and ensuring business continuity.

E. Evaluating Antivirus Solutions: Navigating the Landscape of Cybersecurity Defenses

Selecting the right antivirus solution is a critical step in safeguarding your digital environment against a diverse range of threats. With the cybersecurity landscape continually evolving, evaluating antivirus solutions has become a complex task. This in-depth exploration delves into the key considerations and methodologies for assessing antivirus solutions, ensuring that you make an informed decision to protect your digital assets and data effectively.

1. Effectiveness in Threat Detection and Prevention

The primary goal of any antivirus solution is to detect and prevent malware and cyber threats. Key factors to consider in evaluating effectiveness include:

- **Detection Rates**: Assess the antivirus solution's ability to detect known threats by checking its detection rates in independent tests and third-party reviews.

- **Zero-Day Protection**: Determine how well the antivirus can handle zero-day threats (newly emerging threats without known signatures). This often involves heuristic analysis and behavioral monitoring.

- **False Positives and Negatives**: Evaluate the solution's false positive and false negative rates. Striking the right balance between these two is crucial to minimize both missed threats and unnecessary alerts.

2. Resource Usage and Performance Impact

Antivirus solutions should protect your system without significantly degrading its performance. Consider:

- **Resource Usage**: Evaluate how much system resources (CPU, memory, disk) the antivirus consumes during scanning and real-time protection. Heavily resource-intensive solutions can impact system performance.

- **Scanning Speed**: Assess how quickly the antivirus can scan your system for threats. Sluggish scanning can disrupt user productivity.

- **Impact on Boot Time**: Examine whether the antivirus solution affects the boot time of your system.

3. Ease of Management and User Experience

Usability and ease of management are crucial, particularly for organizations with multiple endpoints. Consider:

- **User Interface**: Evaluate the antivirus software's user interface for user-friendliness and intuitiveness. A confusing or overly complex interface can lead to configuration errors.

- **Centralized Management**: For businesses, check if the antivirus solution offers centralized management consoles for easy deployment, monitoring, and policy enforcement across multiple devices.

- **Customization**: Look for customization options that allow you to tailor security policies to your specific needs.

4. Updates and Support

Regular updates and support are vital for maintaining the effectiveness of your antivirus solution:

- **Virus Definitions**: Ensure that the antivirus provider regularly updates virus definitions to stay current with emerging threats.

- **Software Updates**: Regular software updates address security vulnerabilities and improve the solution's performance and functionality.

- **Technical Support**: Assess the quality and availability of technical support, including response times and support channels (e.g., phone, email, chat).

5. Scalability and Compatibility

Consider the antivirus solution's scalability and compatibility with your existing infrastructure:

- **Scalability**: Ensure the antivirus solution can scale to accommodate the needs of your organization as it grows.

- **Compatibility**: Check that the solution is compatible with your operating systems and software applications.

6. Additional Features and Value-Added Services

Antivirus solutions often offer additional features and services, which can enhance your overall cybersecurity strategy:

- **Firewall**: Some antivirus solutions include firewall capabilities to monitor network traffic and block unauthorized access.

- **Email Security**: Assess whether the antivirus solution provides email filtering and protection against phishing emails, malicious attachments, and spam.

- **Ransomware Protection**: Determine if the antivirus offers dedicated ransomware protection features.

7. Cost and Licensing

Understand the total cost of ownership, including licensing fees and any additional costs for features or services:

- **Pricing Models**: Antivirus solutions may use different pricing models, such as per user, per device, or per year. Choose a model that aligns with your budget and requirements.

- **License Renewal**: Consider the cost of renewing licenses annually or periodically.

8. Independent Testing and Reviews

Look for independent tests and reviews conducted by reputable organizations and cybersecurity experts. These assessments can provide valuable insights into the performance and effectiveness of antivirus solutions.

9. User Feedback and References

Seek feedback from existing users or references provided by the antivirus solution provider. Real-world experiences and testimonials can offer valuable perspectives.

10. Legal and Compliance Considerations

Ensure that the antivirus solution complies with legal and regulatory requirements relevant to your industry or jurisdiction.

11. Trial Periods and Demos

Many antivirus providers offer trial periods or demos, allowing you to test the solution in your environment before making a commitment.

12. Long-Term Strategy

Consider your long-term cybersecurity strategy. Ensure that the antivirus solution aligns with your organization's evolving needs and the changing threat landscape.

By carefully evaluating antivirus solutions based on these criteria, you can make an informed decision that aligns with your cybersecurity objectives and effectively protects your digital assets and data.

Chapter 6

Cybersecurity Best Practices

In an era where our digital presence is intertwined with nearly every aspect of our lives, the importance of cybersecurity best practices cannot be overstated. This chapter serves as a comprehensive guide, delving into the fundamental principles and strategies that individuals and organizations alike should adopt to fortify their defenses against the ever-evolving landscape of cyber threats. From regular software updates to user education and network security, we embark on a journey through the realm of cybersecurity best practices, equipping you with the knowledge and tools to protect your digital world effectively.

A. Regular Software Updates and Patch Management: Safeguarding Against Vulnerabilities

In the dynamic world of cybersecurity, where threats are ever-evolving, the proactive act of keeping software up-to-date and managing patches has become a fundamental pillar of digital defense. Regular software updates and patch management are essential practices to mitigate vulnerabilities that cybercriminals often exploit. In this comprehensive exploration, we delve into the significance, methodologies, and best practices of regular software updates and patch management, equipping individuals and organizations with the knowledge to protect their digital assets effectively.

1. The Significance of Regular Software Updates and Patch Management

The significance of regular software updates and patch management can be summarized in a few key points:

• **Vulnerability Mitigation**: Software updates and patches address known security vulnerabilities, closing the door to potential cyberattacks. Cybercriminals often target outdated software.

• **Protection Against Exploits**: Cyber adversaries frequently exploit known vulnerabilities in software to gain unauthorized access, execute malicious code, or compromise systems.

• **Reduced Attack Surface**: Keeping software updated reduces the attack surface, making it harder for cybercriminals to find and exploit weaknesses.

• **Compliance Requirements**: Many industries and regulations require organizations to maintain up-to-date software and apply patches promptly to protect sensitive data.

2. The Patch Management Process

Patch management involves a structured process to identify, test, and apply patches effectively. Here are the key steps:

- **Identification**: Identify vulnerabilities in your software by monitoring security advisories, vendor announcements, and threat intelligence sources.

- **Assessment**: Evaluate the impact of vulnerabilities on your systems and prioritize patches based on severity and criticality.

- **Testing**: Before deploying patches to production systems, test them in a controlled environment or on non-production systems to ensure they won't disrupt operations.

- **Deployment**: Apply patches to affected systems following a schedule and procedures that minimize disruption to business operations.

- **Verification**: After deployment, verify that patches were applied successfully and that systems remain operational and secure.

- **Monitoring**: Continuously monitor for new vulnerabilities and security updates, and repeat the patch management process as needed.

3. Challenges in Patch Management

Patch management can be challenging for various reasons:

- **Complexity**: Organizations with diverse software ecosystems may find it challenging to track and manage patches for multiple applications and systems.

- **Compatibility**: Patches can sometimes introduce compatibility issues or conflicts with existing software or configurations.

- **Timeliness**: Applying patches promptly is crucial, but organizations may struggle to keep up with the pace of new vulnerabilities and patches.

- **Legacy Systems**: Legacy systems may not receive regular updates or patches from vendors, posing a security risk.

4. Automated Patch Management Solutions

Automated patch management solutions can streamline the process by:

- **Automating Patch Deployment**: These solutions can automatically download, test, and deploy patches to endpoints, reducing the manual effort required.

- **Scheduling**: Administrators can schedule patch deployments during non-business hours to minimize disruptions.

- **Reporting and Monitoring**: Automated solutions provide reporting and monitoring capabilities to track patch status and compliance.

5. Best Practices for Effective Patch Management

To ensure effective patch management, consider the following best practices:

- **Patch Regularly**: Establish a routine for regularly checking for and applying patches. Critical patches should be deployed as soon as possible.

- **Prioritize**: Prioritize patches based on severity, criticality, and the potential impact on your organization.

- **Test Thoroughly**: Test patches in a controlled environment before deploying them in production to avoid unexpected issues.

- **Segment Networks**: Segment your network to isolate critical systems from less critical ones, making it easier to prioritize and test patches.

- **Backup Data**: Regularly back up data to ensure you can recover if a patch causes unexpected issues.

- **Keep Inventory**: Maintain an inventory of software and hardware assets to facilitate patch management.

- **User Education**: Educate users about the importance of not delaying updates or patches and the risks of running outdated software.

- **Automate Where Possible**: Implement automated patch management solutions to streamline the process.

6. The Role in a Comprehensive Defense Strategy

Regular software updates and patch management are integral components of a comprehensive cybersecurity defense strategy. By proactively addressing known vulnerabilities, organizations can significantly reduce the risk of cyberattacks and data breaches. In today's rapidly evolving threat landscape, patch management is not just a best practice; it's a crucial requirement to protect digital assets and ensure the integrity of systems and data.

B. User Education and Security Awareness: Empowering the Human Firewall

In the intricate world of cybersecurity, individuals are often the first line of defense against cyber threats. User education and security awareness programs play a pivotal role in empowering individuals to become vigilant guardians of digital security. This in-depth exploration delves into the significance, methodologies, and best practices of user education and security awareness, equipping individuals and organizations with the knowledge and strategies to fortify their human firewall against the relentless tide of cyber threats.

1. The Significance of User Education and Security Awareness

User education and security awareness are crucial for several reasons:

- **Human Factor**: Cybercriminals often exploit human vulnerabilities, such as ignorance, carelessness, or gullibility, to breach security defenses.

- **Phishing and Social Engineering**: Many cyberattacks, including phishing and social engineering, target individuals. Educated users are less likely to fall victim to these tactics.

- **Data Protection**: User awareness is essential for protecting sensitive data, both at the individual and organizational levels.

- **Compliance and Regulations**: Many industries and regulations require organizations to provide cybersecurity training and awareness programs to protect sensitive information.

2. Components of User Education and Security Awareness

Effective user education and security awareness programs

encompass various components:

- **Training**: Formal training programs teach individuals about cybersecurity concepts, best practices, and how to recognize threats.

- **Awareness Campaigns**: Ongoing awareness campaigns use various media and communication channels to keep cybersecurity top of mind for users.

- **Simulated Attacks**: Phishing simulations and other security tests help users recognize and respond to threats effectively.

- **Reporting Procedures**: Users should know how to report security incidents and suspicious activity promptly.

- **Policies and Procedures**: Users should be familiar with organization-wide security policies and procedures.

3. Phishing and Social Engineering Awareness

Phishing and social engineering are significant threats, and user education is key to mitigating these risks:

- **Recognizing Phishing Emails**: Users should be trained to identify common signs of phishing emails, including suspicious sender addresses, misspellings, and requests for sensitive information.

- **Avoiding Social Engineering**: Awareness programs should educate users on the tactics used by social engineers to manipulate them into disclosing information or taking unauthorized actions.

4. Password Hygiene and Authentication Awareness

Educating users about password hygiene and authentication best practices can prevent unauthorized access:

- **Strong Passwords**: Users should understand the importance of creating strong, unique passwords for each account or service.

- **Multi-Factor Authentication (MFA)**: Awareness programs should promote the use of MFA to add an additional layer of security.

5. Mobile Device Security Awareness

As mobile devices become integral to daily life and work, awareness of mobile security is crucial:

- **App Permissions**: Users should understand app permissions and only grant necessary access to apps.

- **Public Wi-Fi Risks**: Educate users about the risks of using public Wi-Fi networks for sensitive activities.

6. Data Protection and Privacy Awareness

Awareness of data protection and privacy is essential:

- **Data Handling**: Users should know how to handle sensitive data securely, including encryption and secure file sharing.

- **Privacy Settings**: Educate users about privacy settings on social media and other platforms.

7. Reporting and Incident Response

Users should know how to report security incidents and suspicious activity promptly:

- **Incident Reporting**: Ensure users are aware of the reporting procedures and whom to contact in the event of a security incident.

- **Incident Response Training**: Train designated personnel to respond effectively to security incidents.

8. Continuous Reinforcement and Evaluation

Cybersecurity awareness is an ongoing process:

- **Regular Training**: Continuously provide training and awareness activities to keep users informed about evolving threats.

- **Feedback and Evaluation**: Collect feedback from users and evaluate the effectiveness of awareness programs to make necessary improvements.

9. The Role in a Comprehensive Defense Strategy

User education and security awareness are integral components of a comprehensive cybersecurity defense strategy. By equipping individuals with the knowledge and awareness to recognize and respond to threats, organizations can enhance their overall security posture. In a world where the human factor remains a critical vulnerability, well-informed users are the foundation of a resilient human firewall that can withstand the onslaught of cyber threats, protect sensitive data, and safeguard digital assets.

C. Data Backup and Disaster Recovery: Safeguarding Business Continuity

In the ever-changing landscape of cybersecurity, data backup and disaster recovery are not just best practices; they are essential pillars of digital resilience. The ability to protect, preserve, and restore critical data and systems in the face of unexpected events or cyberattacks is paramount. In this in-depth exploration, we delve into the significance, methodologies, and best practices of data backup and disaster recovery, equipping individuals and organizations with the knowledge to ensure business continuity and data integrity.

1. The Significance of Data Backup and Disaster Recovery

Data backup and disaster recovery are critical for several reasons:

- **Data Preservation**: In the event of data loss due to hardware failures, human errors, or cyberattacks, backups ensure the preservation of critical data.

- **Business Continuity**: Disaster recovery plans help organizations maintain operations during and after disruptive events, minimizing downtime and financial losses.

- **Data Integrity**: Backups and recovery measures maintain data integrity, ensuring that information remains accurate and uncorrupted.

- **Compliance and Regulations**: Many industries and regulations mandate data protection, including regular backups and disaster recovery planning.

2. Components of Data Backup and Disaster Recovery

Effective data backup and disaster recovery strategies encompass several components:

- **Backup Policies**: Establish clear policies outlining what data should be backed up, how often, and where backups should be stored.

- **Backup Solutions**: Employ robust backup solutions that facilitate automatic and regular data backups, including both on-premises and cloud-based options.

- **Data Restoration Procedures**: Develop procedures and plans for restoring data quickly and efficiently in the event of data loss or system failures.

- **Disaster Recovery Plans**: Create comprehensive disaster recovery plans that detail how to resume operations after disruptive events, including hardware failures, natural disasters, and cyberattacks.

- **Testing and Training**: Regularly test backup and recovery procedures and provide training to staff to ensure they can respond effectively during incidents.

3. Data Backup Methods

Data can be backed up using various methods, each with its own advantages and considerations:

- **Full Backups**: Full backups copy all data and files, making them suitable for complete data restoration but potentially resource-intensive.

- **Incremental Backups**: Incremental backups only copy data that has changed since the last backup, reducing storage requirements and backup times.

- **Differential Backups**: Differential backups copy data that has changed since the last full backup, providing a balance between full and incremental backups.

- **Snapshot Backups**: Snapshot backups capture the state of a system at a specific point in time, allowing for quick system recovery.

4. Disaster Recovery Planning

Effective disaster recovery planning involves the following steps:

- **Risk Assessment**: Identify potential risks and threats that could disrupt operations or lead to data loss.

- **Business Impact Analysis**: Assess the impact of potential disasters on critical business functions and prioritize recovery efforts accordingly.

- **Recovery Objectives**: Define recovery time objectives (RTOs) and recovery point objectives (RPOs) to establish the acceptable downtime and data loss limits.

- **Backup and Recovery Strategies**: Develop backup and recovery strategies that align with business needs and objectives.

- **Testing and Drills**: Regularly test disaster recovery

plans through simulation exercises and drills to identify weaknesses and improve preparedness.

5. Offsite Backup and Redundancy

To enhance data resilience, consider:

- **Offsite Backup**: Store backups in offsite locations to protect against on-premises disasters like fires, floods, or theft.

- **Redundancy**: Implement data redundancy by maintaining backups in multiple locations or using redundant hardware to minimize data loss and downtime.

6. Data Encryption and Security

To protect data during backup and recovery:

- **Encryption**: Encrypt data during transmission and storage to ensure its confidentiality and integrity.

- **Access Control**: Implement strict access control measures to prevent unauthorized access to backup systems and data.

7. Cloud-Based Backup and Disaster Recovery

Cloud-based solutions offer scalability, accessibility, and cost-efficiency for backup and recovery:

- **Data Storage**: Use cloud storage solutions to securely

store backups offsite.

- **Disaster Recovery as a Service (DRaaS)**: DRaaS providers offer disaster recovery solutions in the cloud, simplifying recovery efforts.

8. Compliance and Legal Considerations

Ensure that backup and disaster recovery plans comply with industry regulations and legal requirements related to data protection and retention.

9. The Role in a Comprehensive Defense Strategy

Data backup and disaster recovery are integral components of a comprehensive cybersecurity defense strategy. In an era where data is a valuable asset and business continuity is paramount, organizations must invest in robust backup and recovery measures. By protecting data, ensuring its availability, and preparing for the unexpected, organizations can navigate the complex cybersecurity landscape with resilience and confidence, safeguarding their operations, reputation, and digital assets.

D. Network Security and Intrusion Detection: Fortifying Digital Perimeters

In the realm of cybersecurity, safeguarding network infrastructure is paramount. Network security and intrusion detection serve as the front lines of defense against a multitude of cyber threats and vulnerabilities. In this in-depth exploration, we delve into the significance, methodologies, and best practices of network security and intrusion detection, equipping individuals and organizations with the knowledge to protect their digital perimeters effectively.

1. The Significance of Network Security and Intrusion Detection

Network security and intrusion detection play pivotal roles for several reasons:

- **Digital Perimeter Protection**: They guard the digital perimeters of organizations, where cyber adversaries often target vulnerabilities to gain unauthorized access.

- **Data Protection**: Network security measures ensure the confidentiality, integrity, and availability of sensitive data and resources.

- **Threat Mitigation**: Intrusion detection identifies and responds to suspicious activities, mitigating threats before they lead to data breaches or system compromise.

- **Compliance and Regulations**: Many industries and regulations mandate robust network security measures and intrusion detection to protect sensitive information.

2. Components of Network Security

Effective network security encompasses multiple components:

- **Firewalls**: Firewalls serve as gatekeepers, filtering incoming and outgoing network traffic to allow or deny access based on predefined rules.

- **Intrusion Detection Systems (IDS) and Intrusion Prevention Systems (IPS)**: IDS and IPS monitor network traffic for suspicious activities and take action to block or alert on potential threats.

- **Access Control**: Implement access control policies and mechanisms to restrict network access to authorized users and devices.

- **Virtual Private Networks (VPNs)**: Use VPNs to secure communication between remote users or offices over public networks.

- **Security Policies**: Develop and enforce network security policies that dictate acceptable use, password requirements, and incident response procedures.

3. Intrusion Detection Methods

Intrusion detection involves several methods:

- **Signature-Based Detection**: This method uses

predefined signatures or patterns to identify known threats and vulnerabilities.

- **Anomaly-Based Detection**: Anomaly detection relies on baseline behavior models to identify deviations that may indicate intrusions or anomalies.

- **Heuristic-Based Detection**: Heuristic analysis looks for behaviors that match known intrusion patterns or tactics used by cyber adversaries.

- **Behavioral Analysis**: Behavioral analysis monitors network traffic and user behavior for unusual patterns or deviations from the norm.

4. Network Segmentation

Network segmentation is a critical strategy:

- **VLANs (Virtual Local Area Networks)**: Segmentation divides a network into smaller VLANs, limiting lateral movement for attackers.

- **Subnetting**: Subnetting separates a network into smaller subnetworks, making it harder for attackers to traverse the entire network.

5. Intrusion Detection Challenges

Intrusion detection can be challenging due to various factors:

- **False Positives**: Overly sensitive detection systems can generate false alerts, potentially leading to alert fatigue.

- **Evasion Techniques**: Attackers employ evasion techniques to bypass detection systems.

- **Encryption**: Encrypted traffic can hide malicious activities, making detection more challenging.

- **Scale**: In large networks, monitoring and analyzing all traffic can be resource-intensive.

6. Continuous Monitoring and Threat Intelligence

Regularly monitoring network traffic and staying updated on the threat landscape are crucial:

- **Security Information and Event Management (SIEM)**: SIEM systems centralize logs and security events for analysis.

- **Threat Intelligence Feeds**: Access threat intelligence feeds to stay informed about emerging threats and tactics.

7. Response and Mitigation

Intrusion detection is most effective when coupled with response and mitigation:

- **Incident Response Plans**: Develop and regularly test

incident response plans to react swiftly to detected intrusions.

- **Automated Responses**: Implement automated responses to block or isolate suspicious activities.

8. The Role in a Comprehensive Defense Strategy

Network security and intrusion detection are integral components of a comprehensive cybersecurity defense strategy. By fortifying digital perimeters, monitoring for suspicious activities, and responding promptly to threats, organizations can bolster their resilience against a multitude of cyber threats. In an era where network breaches can result in significant financial and reputational damage, robust network security and intrusion detection measures are essential for protecting sensitive data, critical systems, and digital assets.

E. Cyber Hygiene for Individuals and Organizations: Building Strong Digital Immunity

In the digital age, practicing good cyber hygiene is akin to maintaining personal and organizational health. Just as regular exercise, a balanced diet, and proper hygiene are essential for physical well-being, adopting cybersecurity best practices is crucial for safeguarding against digital threats. In this comprehensive exploration, we delve into the significance, methodologies, and best practices of cyber hygiene for both individuals and organizations, empowering them to build strong digital immunity in a constantly evolving threat landscape.

1. The Significance of Cyber Hygiene

Cyber hygiene is significant for several reasons:

- **Preventing Data Breaches**: Cyber hygiene helps individuals and organizations avoid falling victim to cyberattacks that can result in data breaches and financial losses.

- **Mitigating Risks**: Adhering to cybersecurity best practices mitigates the risk of malware infections, identity theft, and unauthorized access.

- **Preserving Reputation**: Good cyber hygiene safeguards personal and organizational reputation, as breaches can damage trust and credibility.

- **Compliance and Regulations**: Many industries and regulations mandate specific cybersecurity practices to protect sensitive information.

2. Cyber Hygiene for Individuals

For individuals, cyber hygiene entails the following practices:

- **Password Management**: Use strong, unique passwords for each online account and consider using a password manager.

- **Two-Factor Authentication (2FA)**: Enable 2FA whenever possible to add an extra layer of security to accounts.

- **Phishing Awareness**: Learn to recognize phishing attempts and avoid clicking on suspicious links or providing personal information.

- **Software Updates**: Regularly update operating systems, applications, and devices to patch known vulnerabilities.

- **Secure Wi-Fi**: Secure home Wi-Fi networks with strong passwords and encryption protocols.

- **Data Backup**: Regularly back up important data to prevent data loss in case of ransomware or hardware failures.

- **Safe Browsing**: Avoid visiting suspicious websites and be cautious when downloading files or clicking on ads.

- **Email Security**: Be wary of unsolicited emails and attachments, especially those requesting personal or financial information.

3. Cyber Hygiene for Organizations

Organizations must adopt comprehensive cyber hygiene practices:

- **Security Policies**: Develop and enforce clear cybersecurity policies that dictate acceptable use, access controls, and incident response procedures.

- **Employee Training**: Provide cybersecurity training and awareness programs for employees to educate them about threats and best practices.

- **Access Control**: Implement strong access controls to limit user privileges and restrict access to sensitive data.

- **Patch Management**: Regularly apply software updates and patches to protect against known vulnerabilities.

- **Firewalls and Intrusion Detection**: Use firewalls and intrusion detection systems to protect networks from unauthorized access.

- **Incident Response Plans**: Develop and test incident response plans to react swiftly to security incidents.

- **Data Encryption**: Encrypt sensitive data during storage, transmission, and on mobile devices.

- **Third-Party Risk Management**: Assess and manage the cybersecurity risks associated with third-party vendors and partners.

4. Security Awareness Training

Security awareness training is essential for both individuals and organizations:

- **Phishing Simulations**: Conduct regular phishing simulations to educate users about the dangers of phishing and how to recognize phishing attempts.

- **Ongoing Education**: Stay updated on emerging threats and educate users about new attack techniques and vulnerabilities.

5. Regular Audits and Assessments

Regularly assess and audit cybersecurity measures:

- **Vulnerability Scanning**: Conduct vulnerability scans and assessments to identify and remediate security weaknesses.

- **Penetration Testing**: Hire ethical hackers to conduct penetration tests to identify vulnerabilities before cybercriminals can exploit them.

6. Cyber Hygiene as a Habit

Cyber hygiene should become a habit:

- **Consistency**: Make good cyber hygiene practices a routine part of daily life or organizational culture.

- **Adaptability**: Stay flexible and adapt to evolving cyber threats and best practices.

- **Collaboration**: Promote a culture of cybersecurity collaboration and reporting.

7. The Role in a Comprehensive Defense Strategy

Cyber hygiene is an integral component of a comprehensive cybersecurity defense strategy. By adhering to these practices, individuals and organizations can create a strong digital immune system that defends against a wide range of threats. In a world where cyberattacks are a constant and evolving threat, adopting good cyber hygiene is essential for protecting sensitive data, critical systems, and digital assets.

Chapter 7

Responding to Malware Incidents

In the ever-evolving landscape of cybersecurity, the inevitability of encountering malware incidents underscores the paramount importance of a well-defined and agile response strategy. This chapter serves as a comprehensive guide to responding to malware incidents, providing individuals and organizations with the knowledge and tactics needed to swiftly and effectively counter cyber threats. From incident response plans to data breach notifications, we embark on a journey to understand, mitigate, and recover from malware incidents, ensuring that the digital fortifications remain resilient in the face of adversity.

A. Incident Response Plans and Procedures: Navigating the Chaos with Precision

In the world of cybersecurity, the inevitability of security incidents underscores the importance of having a well-structured incident response plan and procedures in place. These plans serve as the guiding framework for organizations to swiftly and effectively respond to security breaches, minimizing damage and downtime. In this comprehensive exploration, we delve into the significance, components, and best practices of incident response plans and procedures, empowering individuals and organizations to navigate the chaos of security incidents with precision and resilience.

1. The Significance of Incident Response Plans

Incident response plans are crucial for several reasons:

- **Rapid Mitigation**: They provide a structured approach to quickly mitigate security incidents, reducing the potential impact.

- **Minimized Downtime**: A well-executed response plan helps minimize downtime and disruption to business operations.

- **Damage Control**: Plans help contain and limit the damage, reducing the potential financial and reputational losses.

- **Legal and Regulatory Compliance**: In many industries, incident response plans are required to comply with data protection laws and industry regulations.

2. Components of an Incident Response Plan

A comprehensive incident response plan typically includes the following components:

- **Incident Response Team**: Define roles and

responsibilities for team members who will lead and execute the response.

- **Incident Classification**: Establish criteria for classifying the severity and impact of incidents.

- **Incident Reporting**: Outline procedures for reporting incidents, including who to contact and how to initiate the response process.

- **Initial Assessment**: Conduct an initial assessment to determine the nature and scope of the incident.

- **Containment Strategies**: Define strategies for containing and isolating the incident to prevent further damage.

- **Eradication and Recovery**: Develop procedures for removing the threat, restoring affected systems, and verifying their integrity.

- **Communication Plan**: Specify who should be informed about the incident, including internal stakeholders, external partners, and authorities if necessary.

- **Forensic Analysis**: Describe procedures for collecting and preserving evidence for forensic analysis and potential legal action.

- **Documentation**: Maintain detailed records of the

incident, including actions taken, findings, and lessons learned.

3. Incident Response Procedures

Incident response procedures detail how to respond to specific types of incidents. These procedures should be customized to an organization's needs and may include:

- **Malware Infections**: Procedures for identifying, isolating, and removing malware from affected systems.

- **Data Breaches**: Steps for investigating data breaches, notifying affected parties, and complying with data protection regulations.

- **Denial of Service (DoS) Attacks**: Response actions to mitigate the impact of DoS attacks on network resources.

- **Insider Threats**: Procedures for investigating and mitigating threats from within the organization.

4. Preparation and Planning

Effective incident response requires thorough preparation:

- **Testing and Drills**: Regularly test and update incident response plans through tabletop exercises and drills.

- **Training**: Provide training to incident response team members to ensure they understand their roles and responsibilities.

- **Tools and Technology**: Invest in tools and technology that support incident detection, response, and recovery.

5. Legal and Ethical Considerations

Consider legal and ethical aspects when responding to incidents:

- **Data Privacy**: Comply with data privacy regulations when handling and reporting incidents involving personal data.

- **Chain of Custody**: Maintain a secure chain of custody for evidence collected during forensic analysis.

- **Legal Counsel**: Involve legal counsel when necessary, especially for incidents that may result in legal action.

6. Communication and Notification

Effective communication is critical:

- **Internal Communication**: Keep internal stakeholders informed about the incident's status and impact.

- **External Communication**: Notify affected parties, such as customers or partners, in accordance with legal requirements and ethical considerations.

- **Law Enforcement and Authorities**: Cooperate with law enforcement and regulatory authorities as needed.

7. Continuous Improvement

Incident response plans should be living documents:

- **Post-Incident Analysis**: Conduct a post-incident analysis to evaluate the response and identify areas for improvement.

- **Update and Refine**: Update the incident response plan based on lessons learned from each incident.

8. The Role in a Comprehensive Defense Strategy

Incident response plans and procedures are integral components of a comprehensive cybersecurity defense strategy. They provide organizations with a structured approach to addressing security incidents and minimizing their impact. In a landscape where cyber threats are a constant and evolving danger, a well-prepared incident response team and a robust plan can mean the difference between rapid recovery and extensive damage.

B. Identifying and Isolating Infected Systems: The Key to Containing Malware Incidents

When a malware incident strikes, swift and precise action is crucial to minimize damage and prevent the infection from spreading further. This chapter focuses on the critical steps of identifying and isolating infected systems, two fundamental aspects of incident response. By effectively pinpointing compromised devices and isolating them from the network, organizations can halt the malware's advance and initiate recovery, ultimately safeguarding their digital assets and reputation.

1. Identifying Infected Systems

Identifying infected systems is the first step in responding to a malware incident:

- **Security Information and Event Management (SIEM) Tools**: SIEM tools centralize logs and security events, helping organizations identify abnormal or suspicious activities.

- **Endpoint Detection and Response (EDR) Solutions**: EDR solutions provide real-time visibility into endpoints, allowing for the detection of unusual behavior and indicators of compromise.

- **Network Traffic Analysis**: Analyzing network traffic can reveal anomalies, communication with malicious domains, or unusual patterns that may indicate an infection.

- **Antivirus and Anti-Malware Scans**: Regular antivirus and anti-malware scans can detect and flag infected systems.

- **User Reports**: Encourage users to report unusual

system behavior promptly.

- **Incident Response Team**: Collaborate with the incident response team to collect and analyze information.

- **Forensic Analysis**: If necessary, perform forensic analysis to identify the extent of the infection and potential entry points.

2. Isolating Infected Systems

Once infected systems are identified, isolating them from the network is imperative:

- **Network Segmentation**: Use network segmentation to isolate affected systems from the rest of the network, limiting the malware's lateral movement.

- **Firewall Rules**: Adjust firewall rules to block communication to and from infected systems.

- **Disconnect from Network**: Physically disconnect infected devices from the network to prevent further data exfiltration or malware propagation.

- **Virtual LANs (VLANs)**: Place affected devices on isolated VLANs to contain the infection.

- **Shut Down or Quarantine**: In extreme cases, shut down or quarantine infected systems to prevent any further malicious activity.

3. Challenges in Identifying and Isolating Infected Systems

Identifying and isolating infected systems can be challenging due to various factors:

- **Stealthy Malware**: Advanced malware may attempt to hide its presence or evade detection.

- **False Positives**: Overly aggressive isolation measures can lead to false positives, disrupting legitimate operations.

- **User Impact**: Isolating systems may impact users or business processes, requiring a balance between security and business continuity.

- **Remote and Mobile Devices**: Identifying and isolating remote or mobile devices that are off-network can be more complex.

4. Coordination and Communication

Effective coordination and communication are crucial:

- **Incident Response Team**: The incident response team should coordinate the identification and isolation efforts.

- **Stakeholder Communication**: Keep stakeholders informed about the status of the incident and actions taken.

- **Documentation**: Maintain detailed records of the identification and isolation processes for post-incident analysis.

5. Restoring and Recovering Infected Systems

After isolating infected systems, organizations must focus on restoring and recovering them:

- **Malware Removal**: Remove the malware from infected systems using appropriate tools and techniques.

- **System Integrity Verification**: Verify the integrity of affected systems to ensure they are clean and safe for use.

- **Patch and Update**: Apply necessary patches and updates to address vulnerabilities that may have been exploited.

- **Data Restoration**: Restore data from backups to ensure minimal data loss.

- **User Education**: Educate users about the incident, the importance of reporting, and best practices to prevent future infections.

6. The Role in a Comprehensive Defense Strategy

Identifying and isolating infected systems are integral components of a comprehensive cybersecurity defense strategy. They are the frontline actions that help prevent malware from wreaking havoc across an organization's network. In a world where cyber threats are persistent and fast-evolving, the ability to swiftly and effectively identify and isolate infected systems is a critical skill that can mean the difference between containment and widespread damage.

C. Data Breach Notification and Compliance: Navigating the Legal and Ethical Terrain

In the complex and highly regulated realm of cybersecurity, data breach notification and compliance play pivotal roles in safeguarding individual privacy and ensuring organizations adhere to legal and ethical standards. This chapter explores the intricacies of data breach notification and compliance, elucidating the significance, regulatory frameworks, and best practices that guide organizations in their commitment to transparency and accountability when a data breach occurs.

1. The Significance of Data Breach Notification

Data breach notification serves several critical purposes:

• **Transparency**: It fosters transparency by informing affected individuals and stakeholders about the breach, helping them take protective measures.

• **Accountability**: It holds organizations accountable for protecting sensitive data and complying with data protection laws.

- **Mitigating Harm**: Early notification can help individuals take action to mitigate potential harm, such as changing passwords or monitoring their financial accounts.

- **Compliance**: Compliance with data breach notification laws and regulations is often mandatory, with severe penalties for non-compliance.

2. Regulatory Frameworks

Data breach notification laws and regulations vary by jurisdiction but generally cover the following aspects:

- **Notification Thresholds**: Define the criteria for when organizations are required to notify affected individuals and authorities.

- **Timeline**: Specify the timeframe within which notifications must be sent, typically ranging from a few days to a month after discovering the breach.

- **Notification Content**: Outline the required content of breach notifications, including a description of the breach, affected data types, and recommended actions.

- **Notification Recipients**: Identify the parties to whom notifications must be sent, which may include affected individuals, regulatory authorities, and credit reporting agencies.

3. Compliance Challenges

Achieving compliance with data breach notification laws can be challenging due to various factors:

- **Complexity**: Navigating the patchwork of different state, national, and international regulations can be complex, particularly for organizations operating across borders.

- **Detection and Reporting**: Organizations may struggle to promptly detect and report breaches, especially if the breach is subtle or takes place over an extended period.

- **Notification Coordination**: Coordinating notifications to multiple parties, including affected individuals, authorities, and third parties, can be logistically challenging.

- **Data Classification**: Identifying which data breaches require notification and which do not can be complex, particularly for organizations with vast datasets.

4. Steps in Data Breach Notification

When a data breach occurs, organizations typically follow these steps for data breach notification:

- **Discovery and Assessment**: Identify the breach, assess its scope and impact, and confirm if notification is required.

- **Notification Planning**: Develop a comprehensive

notification plan, including identifying the affected individuals, preparing notification content, and establishing a timeline.

- **Notification Execution**: Notify affected individuals, regulatory authorities, and other relevant parties within the specified timeframe.

- **Media and Public Relations**: Prepare for media inquiries and public relations responses, maintaining transparency and trust.

- **Internal Investigation**: Conduct an internal investigation to understand the breach's cause and prevent future incidents.

5. Communication Best Practices

Effective communication is vital during a data breach:

- **Clarity**: Ensure breach notifications are clear, concise, and contain relevant information.

- **Timeliness**: Comply with notification deadlines to maintain legal compliance.

- **Transparency**: Be transparent about the scope and impact of the breach without revealing sensitive information that could further compromise security.

- **Support**: Offer support and resources to affected

individuals, such as credit monitoring or identity theft protection services.

6. Post-Breach Evaluation and Remediation

After a data breach, organizations should conduct a post-breach evaluation:

- **Root Cause Analysis**: Identify the root causes of the breach and take steps to remediate vulnerabilities.

- **Continuous Improvement**: Use lessons learned to improve security measures and incident response procedures.

7. The Role in a Comprehensive Defense Strategy

Data breach notification and compliance are integral components of a comprehensive cybersecurity defense strategy. They provide organizations with the means to respond transparently and responsibly when a breach occurs, safeguarding individuals' privacy and maintaining trust. In an era where data breaches can have far-reaching consequences, organizations that prioritize compliance and effective breach notification demonstrate their commitment to data protection and accountability.

D. Post-Incident Analysis and Remediation: Learning from Adversity to Strengthen Cybersecurity

In the realm of cybersecurity, the aftermath of a security incident offers invaluable opportunities for growth and improvement. This chapter delves into the intricacies of post-incident analysis and remediation, illuminating the significance, methodologies, and best practices that guide organizations in extracting meaningful insights from security incidents and bolstering their defenses against future threats.

1. The Significance of Post-Incident Analysis and Remediation

Post-incident analysis and remediation are critical for several reasons:

- **Learning Opportunity**: They provide organizations with an opportunity to learn from the incident, understand its causes, and identify weaknesses in their defenses.

- **Preventing Recurrence**: Insights gained from analysis enable organizations to remediate vulnerabilities and prevent similar incidents in the future.

- **Improving Cyber Resilience**: By continuously improving cybersecurity measures, organizations enhance their ability to withstand future attacks.

- **Legal and Regulatory Compliance**: Many regulations mandate post-incident analysis and remediation as part of data breach response and compliance efforts.

2. Steps in Post-Incident Analysis

Effective post-incident analysis typically involves the following steps:

- **Incident Identification**: Identify and confirm the occurrence of a security incident, including its scope and impact.

- **Evidence Preservation**: Preserve digital evidence related to the incident, maintaining a secure chain of custody.

- **Root Cause Analysis**: Determine the root causes of the incident, including vulnerabilities, misconfigurations, or human errors that contributed to the breach.

- **Impact Assessment**: Assess the impact of the incident on systems, data, and business operations.

- **Threat Attribution**: If possible, attribute the incident to specific threat actors or attack techniques.

- **Timeline Reconstruction**: Create a timeline of the incident, detailing the sequence of events leading up to and following the breach.

- **Documentation**: Maintain detailed records of analysis

findings, actions taken, and lessons learned.

3. Remediation Strategies

Remediation strategies aim to address the vulnerabilities and weaknesses exposed during the incident:

- **Patch and Update**: Apply necessary patches and updates to address vulnerabilities that were exploited.

- **Configuration Review**: Review and adjust system configurations to eliminate misconfigurations that contributed to the incident.

- **Access Control**: Strengthen access controls and user privileges to prevent unauthorized access.

- **Security Awareness Training**: Provide additional training and awareness programs to educate staff about security best practices and potential threats.

- **Security Tool Enhancements**: Enhance security tools and solutions to better detect and respond to similar incidents in the future.

- **Policy and Procedure Updates**: Review and update security policies and procedures to align with lessons learned.

4. Continuous Improvement

Continuous improvement is a fundamental principle of post-incident analysis:

• **Lessons Learned**: Use insights from the incident to inform cybersecurity strategy and decision-making.

• **Testing and Simulation**: Regularly test incident response procedures and security measures through simulations and exercises.

• **Information Sharing**: Share incident details and lessons learned with the broader cybersecurity community to benefit others and foster collective defense.

5. Cultural Shift

Embracing a culture of learning and improvement is essential:

• **Responsibility**: Foster a sense of responsibility and accountability across the organization for cybersecurity.

• **Communication**: Encourage open and transparent communication about security incidents and their impact.

• **Ownership**: Ensure that incident analysis and remediation are owned by the organization as a whole, rather than a single department.

6. Legal and Ethical Considerations

Consider legal and ethical aspects during post-incident analysis:

- **Data Privacy**: Comply with data privacy regulations when handling and storing incident data.

- **Chain of Custody**: Maintain a secure chain of custody for digital evidence.

- **Transparency**: Be transparent with affected parties, regulatory authorities, and stakeholders as required by laws and regulations.

7. The Role in a Comprehensive Defense Strategy

Post-incident analysis and remediation are integral components of a comprehensive cybersecurity defense strategy. By diligently assessing incidents, learning from them, and taking concrete steps to strengthen defenses, organizations demonstrate their commitment to cybersecurity resilience and adaptability. In a landscape where cyber threats are persistent and evolving, the ability to evolve and improve is a critical asset in maintaining digital security.

E. Legal and Ethical Considerations in Cybersecurity: Navigating a Complex Landscape

In the realm of cybersecurity, legal and ethical considerations are paramount. This chapter delves into the intricate world of legal and ethical aspects of cybersecurity, exploring the significance, frameworks, and best practices that guide individuals and organizations in their efforts to protect data, privacy, and adhere to the rule of law while defending against cyber threats.

1. The Significance of Legal and Ethical Considerations

Legal and ethical considerations in cybersecurity are crucial for several reasons:

- **Compliance and Accountability**: They ensure compliance with laws and regulations governing data protection and privacy, holding organizations accountable for safeguarding sensitive information.

- **Privacy Protection**: Legal and ethical principles protect individual privacy rights and personal data from unauthorized access and misuse.

- **Reputation and Trust**: Adherence to ethical standards helps organizations maintain a strong reputation and build trust with customers and stakeholders.

- **Legal Consequences**: Violations of cybersecurity

laws and ethics can result in legal repercussions, fines, and damage to an organization's reputation.

2. Regulatory Frameworks

Legal considerations in cybersecurity are often governed by a variety of regulations and frameworks, including:

- **General Data Protection Regulation (GDPR)**: GDPR is a European Union regulation that imposes strict data protection and privacy requirements on organizations handling personal data of EU citizens.

- **California Consumer Privacy Act (CCPA)**: CCPA is a California state law that grants California residents certain rights over their personal information.

- **Health Insurance Portability and Accountability Act (HIPAA)**: HIPAA is a U.S. federal law that mandates security and privacy protections for healthcare information.

- **Cybersecurity Laws**: Various countries and regions have enacted cybersecurity laws that require organizations to implement specific security measures and report data breaches.

3. Data Privacy and Protection

Data privacy and protection are core ethical and legal considerations:

- **Data Classification**: Organizations must classify data based on its sensitivity and apply appropriate security measures.

- **Consent**: Obtaining clear and informed consent is often required before collecting and processing personal data.

- **Data Minimization**: Collect and retain only the data necessary for a legitimate purpose.

- **Data Security**: Implement robust security measures to protect data from unauthorized access and breaches.

4. Transparency and Accountability

Transparency and accountability are ethical principles that organizations should uphold:

- **Transparency**: Be transparent with individuals about data collection and processing practices.

- **Accountability**: Take responsibility for data protection and security, and have mechanisms in place to respond to breaches.

5. Incident Reporting and Notification

Legal and ethical obligations often require organizations to report and notify affected parties in the event of a data breach:

- **Notification Timelines**: Laws and regulations specify

deadlines for reporting breaches, typically within a specific timeframe.

- **Content of Notifications**: Notifications must contain specific information about the breach, its impact, and steps affected parties should take.

- **Internal Reporting**: Organizations must have internal procedures for reporting and documenting breaches.

6. Ethical Hacking and Vulnerability Disclosure

Ethical hacking and vulnerability disclosure programs are essential:

- **Ethical Hacking**: Organizations may engage ethical hackers to identify vulnerabilities before malicious actors exploit them.

- **Vulnerability Disclosure**: Establish clear procedures for individuals or security researchers to report vulnerabilities responsibly.

7. Compliance Audits and Assessments

Regular compliance audits and assessments help ensure adherence to legal and ethical standards:

- **Internal Audits**: Organizations should conduct internal audits to assess compliance with security and privacy policies.

- **External Audits**: Third-party auditors may assess compliance with specific regulations or frameworks.

8. Legal and Ethical Dilemmas

Cybersecurity professionals may face ethical dilemmas, such as balancing security with privacy rights or handling sensitive data ethically:

- **Whistleblowing**: Employees who discover wrongdoing within their organizations may face ethical dilemmas related to whistleblowing.

- **Data Handling**: Ethical considerations arise when handling data that may have national security implications or involve sensitive personal information.

9. The Role in a Comprehensive Defense Strategy

Legal and ethical considerations are integral components of a comprehensive cybersecurity defense strategy. They guide organizations in ensuring that their cybersecurity practices align with legal requirements and ethical standards, promoting transparency, privacy protection, and accountability. In a rapidly evolving digital landscape, a firm commitment to legal and ethical principles is essential to maintaining trust, complying with regulations, and protecting sensitive data and individual rights.

Chapter 8

Advanced Threats and APTs

In the ever-evolving world of cybersecurity, the term "advanced threats" and the acronym "APTs" strike fear into the hearts of security professionals worldwide. This chapter embarks on an exploration of advanced threats and APTs, shining a light on the clandestine world of cyberattacks that are both sophisticated and highly targeted. By delving into the intricacies of these threats, we aim to equip individuals and organizations with the knowledge and strategies necessary to detect, mitigate, and defend against these formidable adversaries in the digital realm.

A. Advanced Persistent Threats (APTs): The Apex of Cyber Espionage

In the realm of cybersecurity, Advanced Persistent Threats (APTs) represent the pinnacle of sophistication and stealth in cyberattacks. APTs are not your run-of-the-mill malware infections or opportunistic hacking attempts. Instead, they are orchestrated campaigns by highly skilled threat actors, often with significant resources and a clear agenda. This chapter delves into the intricate world of APTs, exploring their characteristics, tactics, techniques, and the formidable challenges they pose to individuals, organizations, and even nations.

1. Understanding Advanced Persistent Threats (APTs)

An APT is a prolonged and targeted cyberattack in which an adversary with significant resources and expertise infiltrates a specific target, often for espionage, data theft, or intelligence gathering. Several key characteristics distinguish APTs from other cyber threats:

• **Long-Term Engagement**: APT campaigns can span months or even years, allowing attackers to maintain a persistent presence within the target's network.

• **Highly Targeted**: APTs focus on specific organizations, industries, or even individuals, tailoring their tactics to suit their objectives.

• **Stealth and Evasion**: APT actors employ advanced evasion techniques to avoid detection, making them exceptionally challenging to identify.

• **Resource Abundance**: These adversaries often have access to significant financial, technical, and human resources, allowing them to develop custom tools and strategies.

2. Goals and Objectives of APTs

APTs have various objectives, including:

• **Espionage**: Gathering sensitive information, intellectual property, trade secrets, or classified data.

• **Sabotage**: Disrupting operations, damaging infrastructure, or causing financial harm.

• **Cyber Espionage**: Targeting governments, corporations, or organizations to obtain valuable intelligence or proprietary information.

• **Long-Term Persistence**: Maintaining a hidden presence within a network to monitor activities or launch further attacks.

3. Common Tactics and Techniques

APTs leverage a range of tactics and techniques to achieve their goals:

• **Phishing**: A common entry point, APT actors craft highly convincing phishing emails to trick targets into clicking malicious links or downloading malware.

• **Zero-Day Exploits**: APTs may employ undisclosed vulnerabilities (zero-days) to infiltrate systems, as they are unlikely to be patched.

- **Lateral Movement**: Once inside a network, APTs move stealthily, escalating privileges and navigating laterally to reach high-value targets.

- **Custom Malware**: APTs often develop custom malware tailored to their specific objectives, making detection more challenging.

- **Data Exfiltration**: Stolen data is covertly exfiltrated from the target network, often in small, inconspicuous quantities to avoid detection.

4. Attribution Challenges

Attributing APTs to specific threat actors or nations is notoriously difficult due to the use of proxy servers, compromised infrastructure, and sophisticated obfuscation techniques. Even when attribution is attempted, it may remain inconclusive.

5. Mitigation and Defense Strategies

Defending against APTs requires a multi-faceted approach:

- **Threat Intelligence**: Stay informed about emerging APT campaigns and their tactics.

- **Endpoint Detection and Response (EDR)**: Implement advanced EDR solutions to detect and respond to unusual behavior and indicators of compromise.

- **Network Segmentation**: Isolate sensitive data and critical systems to limit lateral movement.

- **Employee Training**: Educate employees about phishing and social engineering risks.

- **Incident Response Plans**: Develop robust incident response plans tailored to APT scenarios.

- **Patch Management**: Keep systems and software up to date to reduce the attack surface.

6. The Ongoing Battle Against APTs

APTs represent an ongoing and relentless challenge in the cybersecurity landscape. As threat actors continually evolve their techniques and exploit new vulnerabilities, organizations and security professionals must remain vigilant, adaptive, and committed to countering these highly advanced adversaries. The battle against APTs is not one that can be definitively won; rather, it is a perpetual struggle to stay one step ahead in the digital arms race.

B. Nation-State Attacks and Cyber Espionage: The Silent Warfare of the Digital Age

In the realm of cybersecurity, nation-state attacks and cyber espionage represent a potent and clandestine form of warfare in the digital age. These campaigns are orchestrated by nation-states or state-sponsored actors with strategic objectives that extend beyond financial gain or chaos creation. This chapter delves into the world of nation-state attacks and cyber espionage, exploring their motivations, tactics, impact, and the complex geopolitical landscape they navigate.

1. Understanding Nation-State Attacks and Cyber Espionage

Nation-state attacks and cyber espionage involve government-backed actors or intelligence agencies conducting covert operations in cyberspace. Key characteristics of these activities include:

• **State Sponsorship**: These attacks are backed by the resources, infrastructure, and intelligence capabilities of a nation-state.

• **Strategic Objectives**: Nation-state actors pursue strategic, political, economic, or military goals, often involving intelligence gathering or influencing global events.

• **Advanced Tactics**: They employ sophisticated tactics, techniques, and procedures (TTPs) to achieve their objectives, often leveraging zero-day exploits and custom malware.

• **Stealth and OpSec**: Maintaining stealth and

operational security (OpSec) is a priority to avoid attribution and detection.

2. Motivations for Nation-State Attacks and Cyber Espionage

Nation-state actors engage in cyber espionage and attacks for various reasons, including:

- **National Security**: Gathering intelligence to protect national security interests, monitor adversaries, or support military operations.

- **Economic Gain**: Stealing intellectual property, trade secrets, and proprietary technologies to boost a nation's economic competitiveness.

- **Political Influence**: Attempting to influence global events, elections, or policies by infiltrating foreign governments and organizations.

- **Geopolitical Agendas**: Pursuing geopolitical objectives, such as territorial disputes or geopolitical dominance, through cyber means.

- **Espionage and Counterintelligence**: Conducting counterintelligence operations to detect and thwart foreign espionage efforts.

3. Notable Examples of Nation-State Attacks

Several high-profile nation-state attacks have garnered attention in recent years:

- **Stuxnet**: Widely attributed to the United States and Israel, Stuxnet targeted Iran's nuclear program, damaging centrifuges used for uranium enrichment.

- **APT28 (Fancy Bear)**: Linked to Russia, APT28 has been associated with various cyberattacks, including the DNC breach during the 2016 U.S. presidential election.

- **Equation Group**: Believed to be tied to the United States, the Equation Group is known for its advanced espionage capabilities, including the use of powerful malware like EquationDrug and GrayFish.

- **APT1 (Comment Crew)**: Allegedly operating on behalf of China, APT1 has been accused of widespread cyber espionage targeting numerous industries.

4. Attribution Challenges

Attributing nation-state attacks and cyber espionage to specific actors or governments is notoriously challenging:

- **False Flags**: Attackers may use deception to make it appear as though another nation or group is responsible.

- **Proxy Servers**: Attacks are often routed through compromised or anonymized servers to obfuscate the source.

- **Shared Tools**: Different nation-state actors may use the same hacking tools, making attribution even more complex.

5. Defense and Mitigation Strategies

Defending against nation-state attacks and cyber espionage requires comprehensive security measures:

- **Threat Intelligence**: Regularly monitor threat intelligence sources to stay informed about emerging nation-state threats and TTPs.

- **Advanced Threat Detection**: Employ advanced threat detection and prevention solutions capable of identifying nation-state TTPs.

- **Network Segmentation**: Isolate sensitive data and systems from the broader network to limit lateral movement.

- **Incident Response Plans**: Develop and test incident response plans specific to nation-state threats.

- **Geopolitical Awareness**: Understand the geopolitical landscape to anticipate potential threats and motives.

6. The Geopolitical Landscape

Nation-state attacks and cyber espionage operate within a complex geopolitical landscape, where the actions of one nation can have far-reaching consequences. The digital realm has become an arena for geopolitical power struggles, with cyber capabilities serving as tools of statecraft and influence on the global stage. Understanding this landscape is essential for organizations and governments alike as they navigate the evolving challenges of the digital age.

C. Zero-Day Exploits and Targeted Attacks: The Precise Arsenal of Cyber Intrusion

In the dynamic world of cybersecurity, zero-day exploits and targeted attacks are the stealthy weapons of choice for highly skilled adversaries. This chapter delves into the intricacies of zero-day exploits and targeted attacks, shedding light on their significance, mechanisms, defensive strategies, and the evolving arms race between attackers and defenders in the digital realm.

1. Understanding Zero-Day Exploits

A zero-day exploit is a cyberattack that takes advantage of a previously unknown software vulnerability or "zero-day." Key characteristics include:

- **Secret Vulnerability**: Zero-days are concealed

vulnerabilities that neither the software vendor nor the public is aware of.

- **Highly Valuable**: Exploiting a zero-day can be lucrative for attackers, as these vulnerabilities are highly sought after in underground markets.

- **Rapid Attack**: Zero-days are typically deployed rapidly after discovery, before vendors can develop and release patches.

2. Targeted Attacks: The Precision Strike

Targeted attacks are cyberattacks directed at a specific individual, organization, or entity. These attacks stand in contrast to opportunistic or indiscriminate attacks. Characteristics include:

- **Custom Tailoring**: Targeted attacks are carefully crafted and tailored to the victim, often involving reconnaissance and research.

- **Stealth and Persistence**: Attackers seek to maintain long-term persistence within the target's network, avoiding detection while they gather valuable data.

- **High Stakes**: Targeted attacks often have high-stakes objectives, such as espionage, data theft, or sabotage.

3. The Anatomy of Zero-Day Exploits and Targeted Attacks

Zero-day exploits and targeted attacks typically follow a sequence of stages:

- **Reconnaissance**: Attackers gather information about the target, including vulnerabilities, network architecture, and potential entry points.

- **Infection**: The attack begins with a vector, often a spear-phishing email or malicious download, which delivers the payload onto the victim's system.

- **Exploitation**: Zero-day exploits are used to take advantage of vulnerabilities in the victim's software or hardware.

- **Command and Control**: Attackers establish a command and control infrastructure within the victim's network to maintain control and gather data.

- **Lateral Movement**: Attackers move laterally within the network to reach high-value targets.

- **Data Exfiltration**: Stolen data is exfiltrated from the victim's network, often in small, inconspicuous amounts to avoid detection.

4. Defensive Strategies

Defending against zero-day exploits and targeted attacks requires a multi-layered approach:

- **Patch Management**: Keep software and systems up to date to minimize the attack surface.

- **Advanced Threat Detection**: Employ advanced threat detection solutions that can identify suspicious behavior and indicators of compromise.

- **User Training**: Train employees to recognize and report phishing attempts and suspicious activity.

- **Network Segmentation**: Isolate sensitive data and critical systems to limit lateral movement.

- **Threat Intelligence**: Stay informed about emerging threats, including zero-days, to anticipate and prepare for potential attacks.

5. The Evolving Arms Race

The battle between attackers wielding zero-day exploits and defenders seeking to protect against them is an ongoing arms race. As attackers continue to evolve their tactics and techniques, defenders must remain vigilant and adaptive. Security researchers, vendors, and organizations must collaborate to discover and patch vulnerabilities promptly, while also developing robust security measures that can withstand targeted attacks.

6. The Future of Zero-Days and Targeted Attacks

As technology advances, the prevalence of zero-day exploits and targeted attacks is likely to persist. Organizations and governments must continue to invest in cybersecurity measures, threat intelligence, and international cooperation to counter these sophisticated threats effectively. The future of digital security depends on the ability to stay ahead of the curve in this relentless battle.

D. Insider Threats and Privilege Escalation: Unmasking the Hidden Risks Within

In the complex landscape of cybersecurity, insider threats and privilege escalation represent a formidable challenge that organizations must confront from within their own ranks. This chapter delves into the intricate world of insider threats and privilege escalation, exploring their motivations, methods, detection strategies, and the vital role of proactive security measures in safeguarding against these insidious risks.

1. Understanding Insider Threats

Insider threats are security risks originating from individuals within an organization who exploit their access, knowledge, or privileges to compromise security or engage in malicious activities. Key characteristics include:

- **Trust and Access**: Insiders have legitimate access to an organization's systems, data, and facilities, often due to their roles and responsibilities.

- **Motivations**: Insider threats may be motivated by a range of factors, including financial gain, personal grudges, ideology, or coercion.

- **Types**: Insiders can be categorized as malicious insiders (those intentionally harming the organization) or inadvertent insiders (individuals who unwittingly cause harm).

2. Motivations and Profiles of Insider Threats

Insider threats may have various motivations:

- **Financial Gain**: Theft of sensitive data, intellectual property, or financial fraud.

- **Revenge**: Disgruntled employees seeking retaliation against the organization.

- **Espionage**: Spying on behalf of competitors, nation-states, or other entities.

- **Ideology**: Individuals motivated by political, ideological, or extremist beliefs.

- **Accidental**: Employees who inadvertently compromise security through negligence or lack of awareness.

3. Privilege Escalation: The Path to Greater Access

Privilege escalation refers to the process by which an attacker or insider exploits vulnerabilities or misconfigurations to gain elevated access privileges within a system, network, or application. Key aspects include:

- **User Privileges**: Attackers or insiders may start with standard user privileges and attempt to elevate their access to administrator or root privileges.

- **Methods**: Privilege escalation can involve exploiting software vulnerabilities, misconfigured permissions, or weak authentication mechanisms.

- **Lateral Movement**: Once privileges are escalated, attackers can move laterally within a network to access critical systems or sensitive data.

4. Detecting and Mitigating Insider Threats

Effectively detecting and mitigating insider threats requires a combination of technical and behavioral approaches:

- **User and Entity Behavior Analytics (UEBA)**: UEBA tools analyze user behavior to identify anomalous activities, such as unusual data access or login patterns.

- **Data Loss Prevention (DLP)**: DLP solutions can help prevent unauthorized data exfiltration.

- **Privileged Access Management (PAM)**: PAM solutions control and monitor privileged access to critical systems and data.

- **Behavioral Monitoring**: Monitor user behavior and access patterns to detect unusual or suspicious activities.

- **Employee Training**: Educate employees about security risks, data handling best practices, and how to recognize and report potential threats.

5. Building a Culture of Security

Organizations must foster a culture of security to mitigate insider threats:

- **Access Control**: Implement the principle of least privilege to restrict access to only what is necessary for job roles.

- **Incident Response**: Develop and practice incident response plans specific to insider threats.

- **Whistleblower Programs**: Establish confidential channels for employees to report suspicions or concerns.

- **Continuous Monitoring**: Continuously monitor user and system activities to identify and respond to anomalies.

6. The Ongoing Challenge of Insider Threats

Insider threats and privilege escalation pose an ongoing and complex challenge to organizations. The dynamic nature of human behavior and evolving attack techniques make it essential for organizations to remain vigilant, adaptive, and proactive in their efforts to detect, prevent, and mitigate these threats. In a world where trust is essential for business operations, managing insider risks is a critical component of a comprehensive cybersecurity strategy.

E. Strategies for Detecting and Mitigating Advanced Persistent Threats (APTs): Fortifying Your Cyber Defenses

Advanced Persistent Threats (APTs) are among the most challenging cybersecurity threats organizations face. These highly sophisticated and targeted attacks can evade traditional security measures and persistently infiltrate networks. This chapter explores strategies for detecting and mitigating APTs, emphasizing the importance of proactive defenses, threat intelligence, and rapid incident response.

1. Proactive Defense Strategies

Proactive defense measures are essential to detect and mitigate APTs before they can cause significant harm:

- **Network Segmentation**: Divide networks into isolated segments, limiting lateral movement for attackers.

- **Least Privilege Access**: Implement the principle of least privilege to restrict user access rights, minimizing potential attack surfaces.

- **Patch Management**: Keep systems and software up to date to mitigate vulnerabilities that APTs may exploit.

- **Endpoint Detection and Response (EDR)**: Employ advanced EDR solutions to monitor endpoints for suspicious behavior and indicators of compromise.

2. Threat Intelligence

Leveraging threat intelligence is crucial for APT detection and mitigation:

- **External Sources**: Subscribe to threat intelligence feeds and services to receive real-time information about emerging APT campaigns.

- **Internal Threat Intelligence**: Collect and analyze internal data to detect anomalies and potential indicators of APT activity.

- **Sharing and Collaboration**: Collaborate with industry peers and security communities to share threat intelligence and insights.

3. Anomaly Detection and Behavioral Analysis

APTs often employ sophisticated tactics that require advanced detection methods:

- **User and Entity Behavior Analytics (UEBA)**: Implement UEBA solutions to identify abnormal user and system behavior indicative of APT activity.

- **Machine Learning**: Employ machine learning algorithms to detect anomalies and patterns associated with APTs.

4. Intrusion Detection Systems (IDS) and Intrusion Prevention Systems (IPS)

IDS and IPS solutions play a critical role in APT detection and mitigation:

- **Signature-Based Detection**: Use signature-based rules to identify known APT attack patterns and malware.

- **Heuristic and Anomaly-Based Detection**: Leverage heuristic and anomaly-based techniques to identify previously unseen APT tactics.

5. Network Monitoring and Packet Analysis

Continuous network monitoring and packet analysis are key for APT detection:

- **Network Traffic Analysis**: Monitor network traffic for unusual patterns, high data volumes, or communications with known malicious entities.

- **Packet Capture**: Capture and analyze network packets to reconstruct APT activity and understand the attack's scope.

6. Incident Response Plans

Having well-defined incident response plans is essential for effective APT mitigation:

- **Preparation**: Develop incident response plans specific to APT scenarios, including roles, responsibilities, and communication protocols.

- **Detection**: Set up systems and processes for detecting APTs, such as automated alerting and monitoring.

- **Containment**: Plan how to isolate affected systems and limit the attacker's movement within the network.

- **Eradication**: Develop strategies for removing APT-related malware and vulnerabilities.

- **Recovery**: Outline procedures for restoring normal operations while ensuring APT persistence is eradicated.

7. Endpoint Isolation and Quarantine

When an APT is detected, rapidly isolate and quarantine affected endpoints to prevent further damage.

- **Disconnecting Affected Systems**: Isolate compromised endpoints from the network to halt communication with the attacker.

- **Forensic Analysis**: Conduct thorough forensic analysis of affected systems to understand the scope of the breach.

8. Threat Hunting

Proactive threat hunting involves actively searching for signs of APTs:

- **Threat Hunters**: Employ skilled threat hunters who specialize in seeking out APT activity within the network.

- **Continuous Monitoring**: Continuously monitor network and endpoint data for signs of APTs.

9. Third-Party Assessments and Penetration Testing

Regular third-party assessments and penetration testing help identify vulnerabilities that APTs may exploit:

- **Penetration Testing**: Engage ethical hackers to simulate APT attacks and identify weaknesses.

- **Red Teaming**: Conduct red team exercises to test the organization's defenses against APT scenarios.

10. Employee Training and Awareness

Train employees to recognize and report suspicious activity and phishing attempts, as they are often the first line of defense against APTs.

11. Collaboration and Information Sharing

Collaborate with industry peers, government agencies, and security organizations to share APT threat intelligence and best practices.

12. Ongoing Assessment and Adaptation

Regularly assess and update APT detection and mitigation strategies to keep pace with evolving APT tactics and the threat landscape.

Mitigating APTs is an ongoing and dynamic process that requires continuous improvement, proactive defenses, and a holistic approach to cybersecurity. By implementing these strategies and staying vigilant, organizations can strengthen their resilience against the persistent and evolving threat of APTs.

Chapter 9

Malware Forensics and Investigations

In the ever-evolving landscape of cybersecurity, the need for meticulous investigation and forensic analysis of malware has become paramount. This chapter delves into the realm of malware forensics and investigations, unveiling the essential techniques and methodologies used to trace the digital footprints left by cyber threats. By understanding how to dissect and analyze malware, we empower ourselves to uncover the hidden secrets of malicious code, attribute attacks to their sources, and bolster our defenses against future cyber threats.

A. Forensic Analysis Techniques: Unmasking the Secrets of Malicious Code

Forensic analysis techniques are the investigative tools used by cybersecurity professionals and digital forensic experts to dissect and understand the inner workings of malware. These techniques play a pivotal role in uncovering the origins, intentions, and impact of cyber threats. This section explores various forensic analysis techniques employed to scrutinize malicious code, investigate cyber incidents, and gather critical evidence for attribution and remediation.

1. Static Analysis

Static analysis involves examining malware without executing it. Key techniques include:

- **File Hashing**: Generating cryptographic hashes (e.g., MD5, SHA-256) of the malware file to identify known samples and detect file modifications.

- **File Metadata Examination**: Inspecting file properties (e.g., timestamps, authorship) to glean insights into the malware's origin and purpose.

- **String Analysis**: Searching for distinctive strings, URLs, or IP addresses within the malware to uncover communication channels and potential command and control servers.

- **Binary Code Review**: Disassembling the binary code to read assembly-level instructions and identify potential malicious functions.

2. Dynamic Analysis

Dynamic analysis involves executing malware within a controlled environment (sandbox) to observe its behavior. Techniques include:

- **Behavioral Analysis**: Monitoring the malware's

actions, such as file system changes, registry modifications, network communications, and process interactions.

- **API Function Calls**: Tracking system calls and application programming interface (API) functions invoked by the malware to understand its functionality.

- **Memory Analysis**: Examining the malware's interactions with system memory, including code injection and data extraction.

- **Network Traffic Analysis**: Capturing and analyzing network traffic generated by the malware to uncover communication patterns and destinations.

3. Memory Forensics

Memory forensics focuses on analyzing the volatile memory (RAM) of compromised systems. Techniques include:

- **Memory Dump Analysis**: Capturing and analyzing memory dumps to uncover running processes, loaded modules, and potential artifacts left by the malware.

- **Malicious Code Injection Detection**: Identifying signs of code injection, rootkits, and hidden processes in memory.

- **Credential Theft Detection**: Scanning memory for evidence of credential theft, including harvested passwords and tokens.

- **Kernel Analysis**: Examining the kernel memory to uncover kernel-mode rootkits and stealthy malware.

4. Reverse Engineering

Reverse engineering involves dissecting and understanding the functionality of malware at a deeper level. Techniques include:

- **Disassembly**: Converting machine code back into assembly language to analyze the malware's logic and operations.

- **Decompilation**: Translating executable binary code into a high-level programming language to facilitate code analysis.

- **Debugging**: Debugging the malware in a controlled environment to trace its execution path, identify vulnerabilities, and understand evasion techniques.

- **YARA Rules**: Creating YARA rules to identify known malware patterns and characteristics in code.

5. Timeline Analysis

Timeline analysis involves reconstructing a chronological sequence of events related to a cyber incident. Techniques include:

- **Log Analysis**: Reviewing system, network, and

application logs to create a timeline of activities leading up to and during the incident.

- **Artifact Analysis**: Examining artifacts on the compromised system, such as file timestamps and registry entries, to establish a timeline of events.

- **Network Traffic Logs**: Analyzing network traffic logs to trace the malware's propagation and communication patterns.

6. Artifact Analysis

Artifact analysis focuses on identifying digital traces left by malware on compromised systems. Techniques include:

- **Registry Analysis**: Examining the Windows Registry for changes made by the malware, including persistence mechanisms and configuration settings.

- **File System Analysis**: Analyzing file system artifacts, such as modified files, created directories, and deleted files.

- **Browser History and Cache Examination**: Reviewing browser history and cache to uncover web-based malware infection vectors and command and control URLs.

7. Malware Attribution

Malware attribution involves identifying the origin or source of a cyberattack. While challenging, attribution may be possible through:

- **Indicators of Compromise (IOCs)**: Collecting and correlating IOCs, such as IP addresses, domain names, and malware artifacts, to attribute attacks to known threat actors.

- **TTP Analysis**: Analyzing tactics, techniques, and procedures (TTPs) used by the malware to link it to known threat groups or nation-state actors.

Forensic analysis techniques empower cybersecurity professionals to dissect malware, uncover its origins, intentions, and capabilities, and develop effective mitigation and remediation strategies. In a digital landscape where cyber threats continually evolve, these techniques remain essential for understanding and countering the ever-present risk of malicious code.

B. Chain of Custody and Evidence Preservation in Malware Forensics

In the world of cybersecurity and digital forensics, ensuring the integrity and admissibility of evidence is paramount. Chain of custody and evidence preservation are fundamental practices that guarantee the credibility of digital evidence in investigations, including those related to malware. This section explores the significance of chain of custody, the techniques for preserving digital evidence, and their critical role in forensic investigations.

1. Chain of Custody: Ensuring Evidence Integrity

Chain of custody refers to the documented and unbroken trail that establishes the control, handling, and location of evidence from the moment it is collected until it is presented in a legal or investigative context. It is essential for maintaining the integrity and authenticity of digital evidence.

Key Aspects of Chain of Custody:

- **Documentation**: Every step of the evidence's journey must be meticulously documented, including who handled it, when, and why.

- **Sealing and Packaging**: Evidence should be secured in tamper-evident containers to prevent unauthorized access.

- **Handling Procedures**: Those who handle the evidence must follow established procedures to avoid contamination or tampering.

- **Logging**: A detailed log or chain of custody form records each transfer or change of possession of the evidence.

- **Authentication**: The chain of custody must be verifiable and reliable to establish the integrity of the evidence.

2. Evidence Preservation

Evidence preservation involves safeguarding digital evidence to ensure its integrity, admissibility, and accuracy throughout the investigation process. This is especially critical in malware forensics, where subtle changes to evidence can impact the analysis and attribution of cyber threats.

Techniques for Evidence Preservation:

• **Forensic Imaging**: Create a forensic copy (image) of the original storage media (e.g., hard drive, server) using specialized tools. The original media should remain untouched.

• **Hashing**: Calculate cryptographic hashes (e.g., MD5, SHA-256) of the evidence to verify its integrity over time. Any changes to the evidence will result in a different hash value.

• **Write-Blocking**: Use hardware or software write-blockers to prevent any write operations to the original storage media during evidence collection.

• **Chain of Custody Documentation**: Maintain thorough records of evidence collection, transfer, and storage, including date, time, individuals involved, and reasons for access.

• **Secure Storage**: Preserve the evidence in a secure environment, such as an evidence locker or digital forensics lab, with controlled access.

- **Tamper-Evident Seals**: Seal evidence containers with tamper-evident seals to detect unauthorized access.

3. Challenges in Digital Evidence Preservation

Preserving digital evidence presents unique challenges:

- **Volatile Data**: Digital evidence can change or disappear if not collected promptly, especially in live systems.

- **Encryption**: Encrypted data may require decryption keys, which should be securely stored and managed.

- **Large Volumes**: Handling and storing large volumes of digital evidence, such as terabytes of data, can be logistically challenging.

- **Remote Locations**: Evidence collected from remote or cloud-based systems requires secure transmission and storage.

4. Legal and Regulatory Considerations

Adherence to legal and regulatory requirements is essential in evidence preservation:

- **Chain of Custody as Admissible Evidence**: Ensuring a proper chain of custody establishes the evidence's credibility and admissibility in legal proceedings.

- **Data Privacy**: Comply with data privacy laws and

regulations when handling evidence, especially if it contains personal or sensitive information.

•   **Laws of Jurisdiction**: Different jurisdictions may have specific rules and requirements regarding digital evidence preservation and handling.

•   **Chain of Custody Documentation**: Prepare documentation that meets legal standards for evidence preservation, including any required certifications.

5. Role in Malware Forensics

In malware forensics, chain of custody and evidence preservation are critical for:

•   **Attribution**: Maintaining the integrity of digital evidence ensures that analysis results are reliable and can be used to attribute cyberattacks.

•   **Legal Proceedings**: If a malware incident leads to legal action, a well-documented chain of custody is essential to demonstrate the legitimacy of evidence.

•   **Incident Response**: Preserving evidence during incident response ensures that critical information is available for investigation and analysis.

Chain of custody and evidence preservation are the foundation of digital forensics and cybersecurity investigations. When executed meticulously, they ensure that the evidence gathered in malware forensics is not only credible but also capable of standing up to scrutiny in a court of law or in any investigation process, ultimately contributing to the pursuit of justice and cybersecurity.

C. Data Recovery and Malware Attribution: Tracing the Digital Footprints

In the realm of cybersecurity and digital forensics, data recovery and malware attribution are crucial processes that help investigators trace the origins of cyberattacks and recover critical information. This section explores the significance of data recovery and the complexities of attributing malware incidents to specific threat actors.

1. Data Recovery: Salvaging Lost Information

Data recovery involves the process of retrieving lost, deleted, or corrupted data from storage devices, even when it appears irretrievable. In the context of malware incidents, data recovery plays a pivotal role in:

- **Restoring Compromised Systems**: After a malware attack, data recovery helps restore affected systems to normal operation.

- **Evidentiary Value**: Recovered data can serve as

critical evidence in forensic investigations, aiding in the identification and attribution of cyber threats.

Techniques for Data Recovery:

- **File Carving**: File carving tools search for file signatures and headers in unallocated disk space to extract deleted or corrupted files.

- **File System Analysis**: Analyzing the file system's metadata can reveal information about deleted or hidden files.

- **Disk Imaging**: Creating a forensic image of a storage device ensures that the original data remains unchanged during recovery attempts.

- **Hexadecimal Analysis**: Examining the raw hexadecimal data of a storage device may reveal traces of deleted or overwritten files.

- **Backup Restoration**: If backups exist, restoring data from backups can be a reliable recovery method.

Challenges in Data Recovery:

- **Overwriting**: Data may be permanently lost if it has been overwritten by new data.

- **Physical Damage**: Physical damage to storage media, such as hard drive platters, can hinder data recovery efforts.

- **Encryption**: Encrypted data may be unrecoverable without access to encryption keys.

- **Data Fragmentation**: Fragmented data may require advanced reconstruction techniques.

2. Malware Attribution: Unmasking the Culprits

Malware attribution is the process of identifying the individuals, groups, or entities responsible for a cyberattack involving malicious software. While achieving definitive attribution can be challenging, it is crucial for understanding the threat landscape and enabling appropriate responses.

Key Aspects of Malware Attribution:

- **Tactics, Techniques, and Procedures (TTPs)**: Analyzing the tactics, techniques, and procedures used by malware can provide clues about the threat actor's identity.

- **Indicators of Compromise (IOCs)**: Collecting and correlating IOCs, such as IP addresses, domain names, and malware signatures, can link an attack to known threat groups.

- **Infrastructure Analysis**: Examining the infrastructure used by attackers, such as command and control servers and email accounts, can lead to attribution.

- **Geopolitical Context**: Attribution may involve

geopolitical considerations, especially when nation-state actors are involved.

Attribution Challenges:

- **False Flags**: Attackers often employ deception techniques to mislead investigators, planting false flags that point to other threat actors.

- **Proxy Servers**: Attackers may route their activities through proxy servers or compromised systems to obfuscate their true origin.

- **Shared Tools**: Attribution becomes complex when multiple threat actors use the same malware or hacking tools.

- **Anonymous Techniques**: Advanced threat actors may use anonymization techniques, such as Tor or VPNs, to hide their tracks.

Attribution Confidence Levels:

- **High Confidence**: When extensive evidence, such as unique TTPs and infrastructure, points to a specific threat actor.

- **Medium Confidence**: When some evidence suggests attribution but lacks conclusive proof.

- **Low Confidence**: When attribution is speculative and lacks substantial evidence.

Legal and Ethical Considerations:

- **False Accusations**: Premature or inaccurate attribution can harm innocent parties and damage international relations.

- **Diplomatic Channels**: In some cases, attribution may be a diplomatic matter rather than a technical one, requiring government involvement.

The Role of Data Recovery in Malware Attribution:

Data recovery can aid in malware attribution by salvaging critical evidence that may have been deleted or hidden by attackers. Recovered data may include:

- **Malware Samples**: Recovered malware samples can be analyzed to identify code signatures, tactics, and infrastructure.

- **Log Files**: Restored log files can reveal details about the attack, such as the timing and methods used.

- **Communication Records**: Recovered communication records, such as emails or chat logs, may provide insights into the threat actor's identity.

- **User Activity**: Data recovery can uncover user activity that may have been erased by attackers, shedding light on their intentions.

Data recovery and malware attribution are intertwined in the investigative process, as they both contribute to understanding the scope and impact of cyber threats. While achieving definitive attribution can be challenging, the combination of data recovery techniques and attribution methodologies enables investigators to piece together the digital puzzle and identify those responsible for cyberattacks.

D. Legal Aspects of Cybercrime Investigations: Navigating the Complex Terrain

The investigation of cybercrimes is a multidisciplinary endeavor that requires a deep understanding of not only the technical aspects but also the legal and regulatory framework. This chapter explores the intricate legal aspects of cybercrime investigations, including the relevant laws, the role of law enforcement, evidence admissibility, and privacy considerations.

1. Cybercrime Laws and Regulations

A crucial aspect of cybercrime investigations is the legal framework that governs them. Laws and regulations can vary significantly by jurisdiction, but several key aspects are common to many legal systems:

- **Computer Crime Laws**: These laws define and classify various cybercrimes, such as hacking, identity theft, and unauthorized access to computer systems.

- **Data Protection and Privacy Laws**: Regulations like the General Data Protection Regulation (GDPR) in Europe and the Health Insurance Portability and Accountability Act (HIPAA) in the United States establish rules for handling personal data.

- **Electronic Communications Laws**: These laws govern issues like wiretapping, interception of electronic communications, and surveillance.

- **Intellectual Property Laws**: Copyright, trademark, and patent laws play a role in cybercrime investigations, particularly in cases involving piracy and counterfeiting.

2. Law Enforcement's Role

Law enforcement agencies are central to cybercrime investigations, but their roles can vary depending on the nature and scope of the cybercrime. Key elements include:

- **Investigation Initiation**: Law enforcement initiates investigations based on reports, tips, or proactive monitoring.

- **Digital Forensics**: Digital forensic experts within law enforcement agencies analyze digital evidence to build cases against cybercriminals.

- **Cybercrime Units**: Specialized units within law

enforcement agencies are dedicated to investigating cybercrimes, such as computer crime units or cybercrime divisions.

- **International Collaboration**: Cybercrimes often cross borders, necessitating international collaboration between law enforcement agencies and INTERPOL.

3. Evidence Collection and Preservation

The collection and preservation of digital evidence are critical in cybercrime investigations:

- **Chain of Custody**: Maintaining a secure chain of custody ensures the integrity and admissibility of evidence in court.

- **Digital Forensics Tools**: Specialized tools and software are used to collect and analyze digital evidence, including disk imaging and memory analysis.

- **Evidence Encryption**: When encrypted data is encountered, law enforcement may need to obtain encryption keys through legal means, such as court orders.

- **Voluntary Cooperation**: In some cases, individuals or organizations may voluntarily provide evidence to assist in investigations.

4. Legal Challenges in Cybercrime Investigations

Cybercrime investigations present various legal challenges:

- **Jurisdictional Issues**: Determining which jurisdiction has authority over a cybercrime can be complex, especially when attackers operate internationally.

- **Privacy Concerns**: Balancing the need to investigate cybercrimes with individuals' right to privacy is an ongoing challenge.

- **International Cooperation**: Coordinating investigations across borders can be hindered by differences in legal systems and diplomatic considerations.

- **Data Retention and Preservation**: Preserving evidence before it is altered or deleted is a time-sensitive challenge.

5. Legal Admissibility of Digital Evidence

Ensuring the admissibility of digital evidence in court is crucial:

- **Rules of Evidence**: Evidence must comply with established rules of evidence, including relevance, authenticity, and hearsay.

- **Expert Witnesses**: Digital forensics experts often

testify to explain the significance of digital evidence to the court.

• **Authentication**: Demonstrating that digital evidence is genuine and has not been tampered with is essential for admissibility.

• **Expert Testimony**: Experts may be required to explain complex technical concepts to judges and juries.

6. Ethical and Privacy Considerations

Cybercrime investigations must also consider ethical and privacy concerns:

• **Respect for Privacy**: Balancing the need for evidence with individuals' privacy rights is crucial.

• **Data Handling**: Investigators must handle sensitive data responsibly to prevent breaches of privacy.

• **Consent and Legal Authority**: Investigators must obtain proper consent or legal authority when accessing private data.

• **Ethical Hacking**: Ethical hacking, or penetration testing, should be conducted within legal and ethical boundaries.

Cybercrime investigations operate at the intersection of technology, law, and ethics. Investigators must navigate complex legal frameworks, address privacy concerns, and adhere to ethical standards to ensure that cybercriminals are brought to justice while upholding individual rights and the rule of law.

E. Case Studies in Malware Forensics: Unraveling the Complexity of Cyber Threats

Case studies in malware forensics provide invaluable insights into real-world cyber incidents, offering a deeper understanding of the techniques, challenges, and methodologies involved in analyzing and mitigating cyber threats. In this section, we delve into several compelling case studies, highlighting the significance of malware forensics in unraveling the complexity of cyber threats.

Case Study 1: Stuxnet - The Cyberweapon that Targeted Iran's Nuclear Program

Background: Stuxnet, discovered in 2010, is one of the most infamous examples of state-sponsored cyber warfare. It was designed to sabotage Iran's nuclear enrichment facilities.

Malware Analysis: Malware forensics experts dissected Stuxnet to uncover its unique characteristics. They found that it utilized multiple zero-day vulnerabilities, sophisticated rootkit techniques, and extensive code obfuscation.

Attribution: While not immediately clear, Stuxnet's complex code and the involvement of multiple zero-day vulnerabilities indicated the work of a nation-state actor, likely the United States and Israel.

Impact: Stuxnet successfully damaged Iran's nuclear infrastructure, delaying its nuclear program. This case underscores the importance of malware forensics in attributing cyberattacks and understanding their geopolitical implications.

Case Study 2: WannaCry - A Global Ransomware Epidemic

Background: In 2017, the WannaCry ransomware spread rapidly, infecting hundreds of thousands of computers worldwide. It demanded a ransom payment in Bitcoin to unlock files.

Malware Analysis: Malware forensics experts analyzed WannaCry's code, revealing its use of the EternalBlue exploit, which exploited a Windows vulnerability. This knowledge was crucial for developing patches and mitigations.

Attribution: Attribution in this case focused on the malware's authors. While the identity of the perpetrators remains unknown, the malware's spread and impact were attributed to a widespread global cybercriminal network.

Impact: WannaCry caused significant disruptions in healthcare, transportation, and critical infrastructure. The case underscores the importance of rapid malware analysis and coordinated responses to global cyber threats.

Case Study 3: NotPetya - A Wiper Disguised as Ransomware

Background: In 2017, the NotPetya malware outbreak, initially thought to be ransomware, turned out to be a destructive wiper designed to cause maximum damage.

Malware Analysis: Malware forensics experts examined NotPetya's code, revealing that it overwrote the master boot record (MBR), rendering infected systems unbootable. This was a key indicator that it was a wiper, not ransomware.

Attribution: Attribution in this case focused on the malware's origin. It was attributed to the Russian military, primarily targeting Ukraine.

Impact: NotPetya disrupted businesses and organizations globally, causing billions of dollars in damages. The case underscores the need for accurate attribution and response strategies in the face of destructive cyberattacks.

Case Study 4: SolarWinds - A Supply Chain Attack

Background: In 2020, the SolarWinds supply chain attack compromised SolarWinds' Orion software, allowing attackers to infiltrate numerous organizations, including government agencies and tech companies.

Malware Analysis: Malware forensics experts analyzed the Sunburst malware, which was used in the attack, to understand its capabilities, communication channels, and evasion techniques.

Attribution: Attribution pointed to APT29, a Russian state-sponsored group. The attack was described as an intelligence-gathering operation.

Impact: The SolarWinds incident highlighted the vulnerability of supply chain attacks and underscored the need for rigorous security measures and comprehensive malware analysis.

Key Takeaways from Case Studies:

- Malware forensics is essential for understanding the technical aspects of cyber threats.

- Attribution can be challenging but is crucial for addressing the geopolitical implications of cyberattacks.

- Rapid analysis and response are critical to mitigating the impact of global cyber threats.

- Supply chain attacks pose significant risks and require comprehensive security measures.

- Effective cybersecurity strategies must encompass technical, legal, and geopolitical considerations.

These case studies demonstrate that malware forensics is not only about dissecting code but also about attributing attacks, understanding their impact, and informing effective responses. They underscore the ongoing need for collaboration among cybersecurity experts, law enforcement, and governments to address the evolving landscape of cyber threats.

Chapter 10

Future Trends in Malware and Antivirus

The world of cybersecurity is in a perpetual state of evolution, driven by the relentless innovation of both malicious actors and the defenders striving to protect digital landscapes. As we embark on this journey into the future, this chapter explores the emerging trends and transformative technologies poised to shape the landscape of malware and antivirus solutions. From the stealthy rise of fileless malware to the transformative power of quantum computing, we delve into the challenges and opportunities that lie ahead, offering a glimpse into the ever-evolving battlefield of cyberspace.

A. Emerging Malware Trends: Unmasking Fileless Malware and AI-Enhanced Threats

As the digital landscape continues to evolve, so too do the tactics and strategies employed by cybercriminals. This section explores two prominent emerging malware trends: fileless malware and AI-enhanced threats. These evolving techniques are reshaping the cybersecurity landscape, challenging traditional defense mechanisms, and demanding innovative approaches to mitigation.

1. Fileless Malware: The Invisible Threat

Overview: Fileless malware represents a significant departure from traditional malware as it operates without leaving conventional traces on the victim's disk. Instead, it resides solely in memory, evading detection by antivirus software designed to scan files.

In-Depth Analysis:

- **Memory-Resident Execution**: Fileless malware runs directly in a computer's volatile memory (RAM), leaving no footprint on the hard drive. This makes it challenging to detect through traditional file scanning.

- **Exploitation of Built-In Tools**: Attackers often utilize legitimate system tools and scripts, such as PowerShell and Windows Management Instrumentation (WMI), to carry out malicious activities. These tools are already present on the system and can be used for lateral movement and data exfiltration.

- **Living Off the Land (LotL)**: Fileless malware leverages trusted processes and applications to camouflage its activities, making it difficult to distinguish from legitimate system behavior.

- **Reduced Signature-Based Detection**: Traditional signature-based antivirus solutions struggle to detect fileless malware due to its lack of executable files and the use of benign processes.

Mitigation Strategies:

- **Behavioral Analysis**: Behavioral monitoring and anomaly detection can identify unusual activities in memory, helping to flag potential fileless malware.

- **Application Whitelisting**: Restricting the execution of specific applications and scripts can prevent unauthorized use of trusted tools.

- **Patch Management**: Keeping systems and applications up to date can mitigate vulnerabilities that fileless malware exploits.

- **Endpoint Detection and Response (EDR)**: EDR solutions focus on detecting and responding to unusual activities, making them more adept at identifying fileless malware.

2. AI-Enhanced Threats: The Rise of Intelligent Adversaries

Overview: The integration of artificial intelligence (AI) and machine learning (ML) into cyberattacks is ushering in a new era of intelligent adversaries. These AI-enhanced threats adapt in real-time, identify vulnerabilities faster, and evade traditional security measures more effectively.

In-Depth Analysis:

- **Automated Attack Decision-Making**: AI-powered malware can autonomously decide on attack strategies, select targets, and adjust tactics based on the evolving security landscape.

- **Faster Threat Discovery**: AI-driven attacks can quickly identify and exploit vulnerabilities, reducing the time window for defenders to detect and respond to threats.

- **Evasion and Stealth**: AI can be used to develop evasive techniques, such as polymorphic malware that changes its code on each infection, making it challenging to detect.

- **Phishing and Social Engineering**: AI-enhanced attacks can craft convincing phishing emails and social engineering campaigns by analyzing target behavior and personal information.

Mitigation Strategies:

- **AI-Powered Security**: Counteracting AI-enhanced threats requires AI-powered defense mechanisms that can match the adaptability and speed of intelligent adversaries.

- **Threat Intelligence**: Continuously monitor emerging AI-driven threats and gather threat intelligence to understand their tactics, techniques, and procedures.

- **User Training**: Educate users about the evolving threat landscape, emphasizing the importance of cybersecurity hygiene and awareness.

- **Multi-Layered Security**: Implement a multi-layered security approach that includes AI-driven threat detection, behavioral analysis, and anomaly detection.

These emerging malware trends, fileless malware, and AI-enhanced threats are indicative of the dynamic nature of cybersecurity. As adversaries become more sophisticated, defenders must evolve their strategies and technologies to stay ahead. The future of cybersecurity lies in harnessing the power of advanced technologies, including AI and ML, to defend against increasingly intelligent and elusive threats.

B. Quantum Computing and Cryptography: A Paradigm Shift in Cybersecurity

Quantum computing represents a transformative technological advancement with the potential to disrupt various fields, including cybersecurity. In this section, we explore the profound impact of quantum computing on cryptography, a cornerstone of digital security. We delve into the principles of quantum computing, its implications for classical encryption methods, and the development of quantum-resistant cryptography.

1. Understanding Quantum Computing

- **Quantum Bits (Qubits)**: Traditional computers use bits as the fundamental unit of data, representing either 0 or 1. Quantum computers employ qubits, which can exist in a superposition of states, enabling quantum computers to process a vast amount of information simultaneously.

- **Quantum Entanglement**: Qubits can be entangled, meaning the state of one qubit is dependent on the state of another, even if they are physically separated. This property enables quantum computers to perform complex calculations efficiently.

- **Quantum Gates**: Quantum gates manipulate qubits, allowing for operations such as superposition and entanglement.

2. Threats to Classical Cryptography

Quantum computing poses significant threats to classical cryptographic methods, including:

- **Integer Factorization**: Quantum algorithms, like Shor's algorithm, can efficiently factor large integers, compromising the security of widely-used encryption schemes such as RSA.

- **Discrete Logarithm**: Quantum computers can solve the discrete logarithm problem efficiently, impacting cryptographic algorithms like Diffie-Hellman and elliptic curve cryptography.

- **Grover's Algorithm**: Quantum computers can perform symmetric key brute-force attacks faster using Grover's algorithm, reducing the security margin of symmetric ciphers.

3. Quantum-Resistant Cryptography

To counter the threat posed by quantum computing, the field of quantum-resistant or post-quantum cryptography has emerged. It aims to develop encryption methods that remain secure against quantum attacks. Key aspects of quantum-resistant cryptography include:

- **Lattice-Based Cryptography**: Lattice-based cryptographic schemes rely on the hardness of lattice problems, which are believed to be resistant to quantum attacks.

- **Code-Based Cryptography**: These schemes are based on the complexity of decoding random linear codes, which quantum computers find challenging to break.

- **Multivariate Polynomial Cryptography**: This approach relies on the difficulty of solving systems of multivariate polynomial equations, which remains computationally expensive for quantum computers.

- **Hash-Based Cryptography**: Cryptographic hash functions play a crucial role in quantum-resistant cryptography, providing security through techniques like hash-based signatures and Merkle trees.

- **Isogeny-Based Cryptography**: This emerging field leverages isogenies between elliptic curves and is believed to offer post-quantum security.

4. Preparing for the Quantum Threat

Preparing for the era of quantum computing requires proactive measures:

- **Migration Plans**: Organizations should develop migration plans to transition from vulnerable cryptographic systems to quantum-resistant alternatives.

- **Quantum-Safe Protocols**: Implement quantum-safe cryptographic protocols to secure data against future quantum attacks.

- **Research and Development**: Invest in ongoing research and development to stay abreast of the latest advancements in quantum-resistant cryptography.

- **Quantum Key Distribution (QKD)**: QKD offers a potential solution for secure communication by leveraging the principles of quantum mechanics to generate unbreakable encryption keys.

5. The Quantum Advantage

Quantum computing also offers potential benefits for cybersecurity:

- **Quantum Key Distribution (QKD)**: QKD enables secure communication channels with unprecedented levels of security. It uses the principle that the act of measuring a quantum state changes it, making eavesdropping detectable.

- **Quantum Random Number Generators**: Quantum-based random number generators can enhance cryptographic security by providing truly random keys and nonces.

The advent of quantum computing presents both challenges and opportunities in the realm of cybersecurity. While quantum threats are on the horizon, the development of quantum-resistant cryptography, quantum key distribution, and quantum-based random number generators offers promising avenues to enhance security in the quantum era. Preparing for this quantum shift requires a forward-thinking approach that combines robust encryption strategies with cutting-edge quantum technologies.

C. Blockchain and Cybersecurity: Fortifying the Digital Fortress

Blockchain technology has emerged as a revolutionary force not only in the world of finance but also in the realm of cybersecurity. In this section, we explore the profound implications of blockchain for cybersecurity, delving into its core principles, applications, and the ways in which it enhances digital defenses.

1. Understanding Blockchain Technology

- **Decentralization**: Blockchains are decentralized, distributed ledgers that operate on a network of nodes. This decentralization eliminates the need for intermediaries, reducing single points of failure.

- **Cryptographic Security**: Blockchains rely on cryptographic techniques to secure data, ensuring data integrity and privacy through techniques like hashing and digital signatures.

- **Consensus Mechanisms**: Blockchains use consensus mechanisms, such as Proof of Work (PoW) or Proof of Stake (PoS), to validate and record transactions. These mechanisms make it computationally expensive to manipulate the blockchain.

- **Immutable Ledger**: Once data is recorded on the blockchain, it becomes nearly impossible to alter or delete, providing a tamper-resistant ledger.

2. Applications of Blockchain in Cybersecurity

Blockchain technology has a wide range of applications in

cybersecurity:

- **Secure Data Storage**: Blockchain can be used to securely store sensitive data, protecting it from unauthorized access and tampering.

- **Identity Management**: Blockchain-based identity solutions provide individuals with greater control over their personal data, reducing the risk of identity theft.

- **Supply Chain Security**: Blockchain enables end-to-end visibility and transparency in supply chains, reducing the risk of counterfeit products and ensuring the integrity of goods.

- **Smart Contracts**: Smart contracts are self-executing agreements with predefined rules. They can automate and secure various processes, such as payments and agreements, without the need for intermediaries.

- **Decentralized DNS**: Blockchain can be used to create a decentralized Domain Name System (DNS), reducing the risk of DNS attacks and domain hijacking.

3. Enhancing Cybersecurity with Blockchain

Blockchain technology enhances cybersecurity in several key ways:

- **Data Integrity**: The immutability of blockchain

ensures that once data is recorded, it cannot be altered or deleted without consensus, making it a powerful tool for preserving data integrity.

- **Secure Authentication**: Blockchain-based identity management solutions offer secure and privacy-enhancing authentication methods, reducing the risk of identity theft and unauthorized access.

- **Decentralization**: The decentralized nature of blockchain reduces the reliance on centralized servers, mitigating the risk of single points of failure and data breaches.

- **Transparent Auditing**: Blockchain's transparency enables real-time auditing and monitoring of transactions and data, making it easier to detect and respond to anomalies.

- **Protection Against DDoS Attacks**: Decentralized applications (DApps) built on blockchain networks are less susceptible to Distributed Denial of Service (DDoS) attacks due to their distributed infrastructure.

4. Challenges and Considerations

While blockchain offers substantial benefits for cybersecurity, it also presents challenges and considerations:

- **Scalability**: Some blockchain networks struggle with scalability, making it essential to choose the right platform for specific cybersecurity applications.

- **Regulatory Compliance**: Compliance with existing regulations and the evolving legal landscape can be complex, particularly for blockchain-based identity solutions.

- **Key Management**: Securely managing private keys is crucial in blockchain-based systems, as the loss or compromise of keys can result in data loss or unauthorized access.

- **Energy Consumption**: Proof of Work (PoW) blockchain networks, like Bitcoin, can have significant energy consumption, raising environmental concerns.

5. The Future of Blockchain in Cybersecurity

The integration of blockchain technology into cybersecurity is poised to play a pivotal role in safeguarding digital assets and data. As blockchain applications continue to evolve, organizations and individuals alike can leverage its capabilities to fortify the digital fortress and protect against an ever-evolving landscape of cyber threats. Whether securing data, enhancing identity management, or ensuring transparent transactions, blockchain has emerged as a powerful ally in the fight for digital security.

D. Preparing for Future Malware Challenges: A Proactive Approach to Cybersecurity

The landscape of malware threats is continually evolving, presenting new challenges and complexities for individuals and organizations alike. In this section, we explore the strategies and considerations for preparing and defending against future malware challenges, focusing on proactive cybersecurity measures and emerging technologies.

1. Threat Intelligence and Information Sharing

- **Continuous Monitoring**: To stay ahead of emerging malware threats, organizations must establish robust threat intelligence programs. These programs involve continuous monitoring of the threat landscape to identify new malware variants and attack vectors.

- **Information Sharing**: Collaborative information sharing among industry peers, government agencies, and cybersecurity organizations is crucial. Platforms like Information Sharing and Analysis Centers (ISACs) facilitate timely threat information exchange.

2. Machine Learning and AI-Driven Detection

- **Behavioral Analytics**: Machine learning and AI-based solutions can analyze user and system behavior to detect anomalies indicative of malware activity. This proactive approach can identify threats even before they trigger traditional signatures.

- **Predictive Analysis**: Machine learning models can predict potential malware attacks based on historical data, helping organizations preemptively fortify their defenses.

3. Endpoint Detection and Response (EDR)

- **Real-time Monitoring**: EDR solutions provide real-time monitoring of endpoints, allowing for the rapid detection and response to malware incidents. They offer granular visibility into endpoint activities.

- **Threat Hunting**: EDR enables threat hunting, where security teams actively search for signs of hidden or sophisticated malware threats that may evade automated detection.

4. Zero Trust Architecture

- **Least Privilege Access**: Implementing the principle of least privilege ensures that users and systems have only the minimal access required for their tasks. This limits the potential impact of malware.

- **Continuous Authentication**: Zero trust architectures employ continuous user authentication, reducing the risk of unauthorized access due to compromised credentials.

5. Security Automation and Orchestration

- **Automated Incident Response**: Security automation tools can respond to known malware threats swiftly, isolating infected systems and blocking malicious traffic before human intervention is necessary.

- **Orchestration**: Orchestration platforms streamline incident response processes by automating workflows and ensuring a coordinated response to malware incidents.

6. Cybersecurity Training and Awareness

- **Employee Training**: Regular cybersecurity training for employees raises awareness of malware threats, social engineering tactics, and safe online practices. Educated users are less likely to fall victim to malware attacks.

- **Phishing Simulation**: Simulated phishing exercises help employees recognize phishing attempts and improve their ability to avoid falling prey to phishing-related malware.

7. Blockchain-Based Security Measures

- **Blockchain for Data Integrity**: Utilizing blockchain for securing sensitive data ensures data integrity, making it tamper-resistant and immune to unauthorized alterations.

- **Decentralized Identity**: Blockchain-based identity

solutions offer secure and user-controlled identity management, reducing the risk of identity theft and credential compromise.

8. Quantum-Resistant Cryptography

• **Preparing for Quantum Threats**: As quantum computing advances, implementing quantum-resistant cryptographic methods becomes imperative to safeguard data from future quantum attacks.

9. Cloud Security

• **Cloud-Native Security**: Leveraging cloud-native security solutions ensures that malware threats are mitigated at the cloud level, protecting data and services hosted in cloud environments.

• **Container Security**: Containerization technologies require specific security measures to prevent malware from infiltrating containerized applications and services.

10. Incident Response Planning and Drills

• **Plan Development**: Organizations should create comprehensive incident response plans tailored to their specific needs, ensuring that all stakeholders understand their roles and responsibilities.

• **Simulation Exercises**: Regular incident response

simulation exercises help teams practice their response to malware incidents and refine their procedures.

Preparing for future malware challenges is an ongoing process that requires a proactive and multi-faceted approach. By staying informed, harnessing advanced technologies, fostering a culture of cybersecurity awareness, and continuously refining incident response strategies, individuals and organizations can fortify their defenses and mitigate the evolving threats posed by malware.

Conclusion

As we draw the final curtain on this journey through these pages, we invite you to reflect on the knowledge, insights, and discoveries that have unfolded before you. Our exploration of various subjects has been a captivating voyage into the depths of understanding.

In these chapters, we have ventured through the intricacies of numerous topics and examined the key concepts and findings that define these fields. It is our hope that you have found inspiration, enlightenment, and valuable takeaways that resonate with you on your own quest for knowledge.

Remember that the pursuit of understanding is an ever-evolving journey, and this book is but a milestone along the way. The world of knowledge is vast and boundless, offering endless opportunities for exploration and growth.

As you conclude this book, we encourage you to carry forward the torch of curiosity and continue your exploration of these subjects. Seek out new perspectives, engage in meaningful discussions, and embrace the thrill of lifelong learning.

We express our sincere gratitude for joining us on this intellectual adventure. Your curiosity and dedication to expanding your horizons are the driving forces behind our shared quest for wisdom and insight.

Thank you for entrusting us with a portion of your intellectual journey. May your pursuit of knowledge lead you to new heights and inspire others to embark on their own quests for understanding.

With profound gratitude,

Nikhilesh Mishra, Author

Recap of Key

As we conclude this comprehensive exploration of computer viruses, malware, and antivirus technologies, it's essential to recap and consolidate the key concepts and insights gained throughout this book. This recap serves as a concise summary of the critical elements you've encountered in your journey towards mastering the realm of cybersecurity threats and protection.

1. Understanding Malware:

- **Definition**: Malware, short for malicious software, encompasses a wide range of software designed with malicious intent, including viruses, worms, Trojans, spyware, and ransomware.

- **Infection Methods**: Malware can infiltrate systems through various infection vectors, such as email attachments, downloads, infected websites, and removable media.

2. Types and Categories of Malware:

- **Viruses, Worms, and Trojans**: These are fundamental categories of malware, each with distinct characteristics.

Viruses attach themselves to legitimate programs, worms spread independently, and Trojans deceive users by masquerading as benign software.

- **File-Infecting Viruses**: These viruses attach themselves to executable files, spreading when infected files are executed.

- **Boot Sector Viruses**: Boot sector viruses infect the master boot record of a computer's storage device, often rendering the system unbootable.

- **Macro Viruses**: These viruses exploit macro scripting languages in applications like Microsoft Office to spread.

- **Ransomware and Spyware**: Ransomware encrypts files and demands a ransom for decryption, while spyware silently collects sensitive information.

3. How Viruses Spread:

- **Infection Vectors**: Malware spreads through multiple vectors, including email attachments, malicious downloads, and infected USB drives.

- **Social Engineering and Phishing**: Cybercriminals use

psychological manipulation to trick users into revealing sensitive information or clicking on malicious links.

- **Drive-By Downloads and Malvertisements**: Malware can be silently downloaded onto a system when visiting compromised websites or clicking on malicious advertisements.

- **Malware Distribution Networks**: Underground networks facilitate the distribution of malware and exploit kits.

- **Zero-Day Exploits**: Attackers leverage unpatched software vulnerabilities to deliver malware before security patches are available.

4. Advanced Malware Analysis:

- **Behavioral Analysis**: Analyzing malware's behavior in a controlled environment to identify malicious activities.

- **Signature-Based Detection**: Recognizing known malware based on predefined signatures.

- **Heuristics and Sandbox Analysis**: Employing heuristics to detect suspicious patterns and running malware in isolated sandboxes for analysis.

- **Machine Learning in Malware Detection**: Using machine learning algorithms to identify and classify new, previously unseen malware.

- **Reverse Engineering Malware**: Dissecting malware code to understand its functionality and create countermeasures.

5. Antivirus Technologies and Strategies:

- **Antivirus Software Features**: Antivirus solutions offer a range of features, including real-time scanning, quarantine, and automatic updates.

- **Real-Time Scanning and Behavioral Analysis**: Continuously monitoring system activity to detect and block suspicious behavior.

- **Heuristics and Cloud-Based Detection**: Using heuristics to identify new threats and leveraging cloud databases for real-time threat data.

- **Advanced Threat Protection**: Combining multiple technologies, such as intrusion detection and application control, to provide comprehensive security.

- **Evaluating Antivirus Solutions**: Assessing antivirus solutions based on factors like detection rates, system performance, and ease of use.

This recap encapsulates the core concepts you've encountered in your journey to master computer viruses, malware, and antivirus technologies. Armed with this knowledge, you are better equipped to understand, detect, and protect against cyber threats effectively, contributing to a safer digital landscape for individuals and organizations alike.

The Ongoing Battle Against Cyber Threats

The digital age has ushered in unprecedented connectivity and convenience, but it has also brought forth a constant and evolving battle against cyber threats. As technology advances and becomes more integral to our daily lives, the landscape of cybersecurity is marked by an ongoing struggle to protect sensitive data, critical infrastructure, and personal privacy. In this section, we delve deep into the multifaceted challenges and the strategies employed in the relentless war against cyber threats.

1. The Ever-Changing Threat Landscape:

- **Adaptation of Threats**: Cybercriminals continuously adapt their tactics, techniques, and procedures (TTPs) to exploit new vulnerabilities and evade detection.

- **Rise of Nation-State Actors**: Nation-state-sponsored cyberattacks have grown in sophistication, targeting governments, businesses, and critical infrastructure worldwide.

- **Advanced Persistent Threats (APTs)**: APTs are prolonged and targeted cyberattacks often associated with espionage or data theft, posing severe challenges to defense.

- **Zero-Day Vulnerabilities**: Exploitation of undisclosed software vulnerabilities (zero-days) remains a potent weapon for threat actors.

2. Emerging Threat Trends:

- **Fileless Malware**: Fileless malware operates in memory, leaving minimal traces on disk and making detection more challenging.

- **AI-Enhanced Threats**: Cybercriminals use artificial intelligence and machine learning to automate attacks and create more convincing phishing scams.

- **IoT Vulnerabilities**: The proliferation of Internet of Things (IoT) devices presents new attack surfaces and potential entry points for cyberattacks.

- **Supply Chain Attacks**: Attackers target software supply chains to compromise widely-used applications and distribute malware.

3. The Role of Cybersecurity Professionals:

- **Cybersecurity Teams**: Skilled cybersecurity professionals play a crucial role in defending against threats, conducting incident response, and mitigating risks.

- **Threat Intelligence**: Gathering and analyzing threat intelligence is essential for staying ahead of evolving threats and vulnerabilities.

- **Continuous Learning**: The fast-paced nature of cyber threats requires cybersecurity professionals to engage in continuous learning and stay updated on emerging trends.

4. Collaboration and Information Sharing:

- **Public-Private Partnerships**: Collaboration between government agencies, private-sector organizations, and international entities is vital for a collective defense against cyber threats.

- **Information Sharing**: Sharing threat intelligence and best practices among organizations helps in early threat detection and response.

5. Ethical and Legal Considerations:

- **Privacy vs. Security**: Balancing the need for security with the protection of individual privacy is a complex ethical and legal challenge.

- **Data Protection Regulations**: Compliance with data protection regulations like GDPR and HIPAA is essential for organizations to avoid legal consequences.

6. Cybersecurity Awareness and Education:

- **User Training**: Educating end-users about safe online practices is critical in preventing successful cyberattacks, especially in cases of phishing and social engineering.

- **Curriculum Development**: Cybersecurity education at all levels, from K-12 to higher education, helps train future professionals and raise awareness.

7. Preparing for Future Challenges:

- **Quantum Computing and Cryptography**: The advent of quantum computing presents both opportunities and challenges in the realm of cryptography and cybersecurity.

- **Blockchain and Decentralized Security**: Blockchain technology offers new approaches to securing data and transactions.

- **Biometric Authentication and Zero-Trust Security**: Advances in biometric authentication and the adoption of zero-trust security models enhance protection.

The battle against cyber threats is ongoing and requires a multi-faceted approach involving technology, policy, education, and international cooperation. Cybersecurity professionals and organizations must remain vigilant, adapt to new threat trends, and employ robust defense mechanisms to safeguard digital ecosystems and maintain the trust of users in an increasingly interconnected world.

Glossary of Terms

Cybersecurity and malware are domains rife with technical jargon and specialized terminology. Understanding these terms is fundamental for navigating the complex world of cybersecurity, protecting digital assets, and combating cyber threats. In this glossary, we provide in-depth explanations of key terms in these fields.

1. **Adware**: Adware is software that displays unwanted advertisements on a user's device. While not always malicious, excessive adware can be disruptive and may compromise privacy.

2. **Backdoor**: A backdoor is a hidden or undocumented method for bypassing normal authentication or security controls in a computer system. It can be used for unauthorized access or control.

3. **Botnet**: A botnet is a network of compromised computers (bots) controlled by a single entity (botmaster). Botnets are often used for various malicious activities, including distributed denial of service (DDoS) attacks.

4. **Brute Force Attack**: In a brute force attack, an attacker attempts to gain access to a system by trying all possible combinations of passwords or encryption keys until the correct one is found.

5. **Cybersecurity**: Cybersecurity refers to the practice of protecting computer systems, networks, and data from theft, damage, or unauthorized access. It encompasses various strategies, technologies, and best practices.

6. **Firewall**: A firewall is a network security device or software that monitors and controls incoming and outgoing network traffic based on predetermined security rules. It acts as a barrier between a trusted network and an untrusted network, such as the internet.

7. **Hacker**: A hacker is an individual with advanced knowledge of computer systems who may use that knowledge for various purposes, including security testing (ethical hacking) or malicious activities (black-hat hacking).

8. **Malware**: Malware, short for malicious software, is software specifically designed to harm or compromise computer systems or data. Types of malware include viruses, worms, Trojans, and ransomware.

9. **Phishing**: Phishing is a cyberattack technique in which attackers impersonate legitimate entities to trick individuals into divulging sensitive information, such as passwords or financial details.

10. **Ransomware**: Ransomware is a type of malware that encrypts a victim's files and demands a ransom for the decryption key. Paying the ransom is discouraged, as it does not guarantee

data recovery and supports cybercriminals.

11. **Zero-Day Vulnerability**: A zero-day vulnerability is a software vulnerability that is exploited by attackers before the software vendor releases a patch or fix. It's called "zero-day" because there are zero days of protection.

12. **Two-Factor Authentication (2FA)**: 2FA is a security mechanism that requires users to provide two separate authentication factors (e.g., password and a one-time code sent to a mobile device) to access an account or system. It enhances security by adding an extra layer of verification.

13. **Endpoint Security**: Endpoint security refers to the protection of individual devices (endpoints) like computers, smartphones, and tablets from cybersecurity threats. It involves antivirus software, intrusion detection, and other measures.

14. **Data Breach**: A data breach is an unauthorized access or exposure of sensitive or confidential data. Breaches can result from cyberattacks, vulnerabilities, or human error.

15. **Cyber Hygiene**: Cyber hygiene refers to best practices for maintaining a high level of cybersecurity, including regular software updates, strong password management, and user education.

16. **Encryption**: Encryption is the process of converting data

into a secure code (ciphertext) to prevent unauthorized access. Only those with the appropriate decryption key can access the original data.

17. **Incident Response**: Incident response is a structured approach to addressing and managing security incidents, including identifying and mitigating threats and recovering from security breaches.

18. **Patch Management**: Patch management involves applying software updates, or patches, to address security vulnerabilities and keep systems protected from known threats.

19. **Social Engineering**: Social engineering is a technique used by attackers to manipulate individuals into divulging confidential information or performing actions that compromise security.

20. **Vulnerability Assessment**: A vulnerability assessment is a systematic process of identifying, quantifying, and prioritizing security vulnerabilities in a system or network to enable proactive mitigation.

This glossary provides a comprehensive overview of key cybersecurity and malware terms, equipping individuals with the knowledge needed to navigate the evolving digital landscape and protect against cyber threats. Understanding these terms is essential for effective cybersecurity practices and decision-making.

Resources and References

As you reach the final pages of this book by Nikhilesh Mishra, consider it not an ending but a stepping stone. The pursuit of knowledge is an unending journey, and the world of information is boundless.

Discover a World Beyond These Pages

We extend a warm invitation to explore a realm of boundless learning and discovery through our dedicated online platform: **www.nikhileshmishra.com**. Here, you will unearth a carefully curated trove of resources and references to empower your quest for wisdom.

Unleash the Potential of Your Mind

- **Digital Libraries:** Immerse yourself in vast digital libraries, granting access to books, research papers, and academic treasures.

- **Interactive Courses:** Engage with interactive courses and lectures from world-renowned institutions, nurturing your thirst for knowledge.

- **Enlightening Talks:** Be captivated by enlightening talks delivered by visionaries and experts from diverse fields.

- **Community Connections:** Connect with a global community of like-minded seekers, engage in meaningful discussions, and share your knowledge journey.

Your Journey Has Just Begun

Your journey as a seeker of knowledge need not end here. Our website awaits your exploration, offering a gateway to an infinite universe of insights and references tailored to ignite your intellectual curiosity.

Acknowledgments

As I stand at this pivotal juncture, reflecting upon the completion of this monumental work, I am overwhelmed with profound gratitude for the exceptional individuals who have been instrumental in shaping this remarkable journey.

In Loving Memory

To my father, **Late Shri Krishna Gopal Mishra,** whose legacy of wisdom and strength continues to illuminate my path, even in his physical absence, I offer my deepest respect and heartfelt appreciation.

The Pillars of Support

My mother, **Mrs. Vijay Kanti Mishra,** embodies unwavering resilience and grace. Your steadfast support and unwavering faith in my pursuits have been the bedrock of my journey.

To my beloved wife, **Mrs. Anshika Mishra,** your unshakable belief in my abilities has been an eternal wellspring of motivation. Your constant encouragement has propelled me to reach new heights.

My daughter, **Miss Aarvi Mishra,** infuses my life with boundless joy and unbridled inspiration. Your insatiable curiosity serves as a constant reminder of the limitless power of exploration and discovery.

Brothers in Arms

To my younger brothers, **Mr. Ashutosh Mishra and Mr. Devashish Mishra,** who have steadfastly stood by my side, offering unwavering support and shared experiences that underscore the strength of familial bonds.

A Journey Shared

This book is a testament to the countless hours of dedication and effort that have gone into its creation. I am immensely grateful for the privilege of sharing my knowledge and insights with a global audience.

Readers, My Companions

To all the readers who embark on this intellectual journey alongside me, your curiosity and unquenchable thirst for knowledge inspire me to continually push the boundaries of understanding in the realm of cloud computing.

With profound appreciation and sincere gratitude,

Nikhilesh Mishra

September 17, 2023

About the Author

Nikhilesh Mishra is an extraordinary visionary, propelled by an insatiable curiosity and an unyielding passion for innovation. With a relentless commitment to exploring the boundaries of knowledge and technology, Nikhilesh has embarked on an exceptional journey to unravel the intricate complexities of our world.

Hailing from the vibrant and diverse landscape of India, Nikhilesh's pursuit of knowledge has driven him to plunge deep into the world of discovery and understanding from a remarkably young age. His unwavering determination and quest for innovation have not only cemented his position as a thought leader but have also earned him global recognition in the ever-evolving realm of technology and human understanding.

Over the years, Nikhilesh has not only mastered the art of translating complex concepts into accessible insights but has also crafted a unique talent for inspiring others to explore the limitless possibilities of human potential.

Nikhilesh's journey transcends the mere boundaries of expertise; it is a transformative odyssey that challenges conventional wisdom and redefines the essence of exploration. His commitment to pushing the boundaries and reimagining the norm serves as a luminous beacon of inspiration to all those who aspire to make a profound impact in the world of knowledge.

As you navigate the intricate corridors of human understanding and innovation, you will not only gain insight into Nikhilesh's expertise but also experience his unwavering dedication to empowering readers like you. Prepare to be enthralled as he seamlessly melds intricate insights with real-world applications, igniting the flames of curiosity and innovation within each reader.

Nikhilesh Mishra's work extends beyond the realm of authorship; it is a reflection of his steadfast commitment to shaping the future of knowledge and exploration. It is an embodiment of his boundless dedication to disseminating wisdom for the betterment of individuals worldwide.

Prepare to be inspired, enlightened, and empowered as you embark on this transformative journey alongside Nikhilesh Mishra. Your understanding of the world will be forever enriched, and your passion for exploration and innovation will reach new heights under his expert guidance.

Sincerely, **A Fellow Explorer**

Notes

Notes

Notes

Notes

Notes

www.ingramcontent.com/pod-product-compliance
Lightning Source LLC
LaVergne TN
LVHW051442050326
832903LV00030BD/3194